The Leadership Imperative

The Leadership Imperative

Leading Biblically in an Age of Fluidity

Scott D. Liebhauser

Foreword by Diane M. Wiater

WIPF & STOCK · Eugene, Oregon

THE LEADERSHIP IMPERATIVE
Leading Biblically in an Age of Fluidity

Copyright © 2017 Scott D. Liebhauser. All rights reserved. Except for brief quotations in critical publications or reviews, no part of this book may be reproduced in any manner without prior written permission from the publisher. Write: Permissions, Wipf and Stock Publishers, 199 W. 8th Ave., Suite 3, Eugene, OR 97401.

Wipf & Stock
An Imprint of Wipf and Stock Publishers
199 W. 8th Ave., Suite 3
Eugene, OR 97401

www.wipfandstock.com

PAPERBACK ISBN: 978-1-5326-3875-6
HARDCOVER ISBN: 978-1-5326-3876-3
EBOOK ISBN: 978-1-5326-3877-0

Manufactured in the U.S.A.   JANUARY 12, 2018

Scripture quotations marked (ESV) are from The Holy Bible, English Standard Version® (ESV®). Copyright © 2001 by Crossway, a publishing ministry of Good News Publishers. Used by permission. All rights reserved.

THIS WORK IS DEDICATED to my wife, Francine. I offer a heartfelt "thank you" for her support, encouragement, and prayers throughout this project. Without her patience during my times of discouragement and her advice while facing mental blocks, I could not have completed this work. Just as this book places a heavy emphasis on biblical servant leadership, I have had a consistent example of this at my side in its fullness. I am reminded of Proverbs 18:22 which states: "He who finds a wife finds a good thing and obtains favor from the Lord." I have indeed found a good thing.

I also want to share my gratitude for my sons, Joshua and Jacob, who are now young adults faithfully working their way through postmodernity in Christ. They have been and will always be a great joy in my life.

I would also like to dedicate this book to the memory of my late father-in-law, Mr. Howard Gane. His humble, gentle spirit and kind heart have left a great impression on me.

Finally, to my Lord and Savior Jesus Christ I owe a debt of gratitude which I can never repay for his grace and mercy bestowed upon this wretched sinner.

Soli Deo Gloria

There is no finally fixed point of reference, no immovable anchor for the soul. We have entered post-modernity; the modernist way of thinking about truth is impossible. Postmodernism, broadly understood, has dispensed with Truth and has replaced it with truths. Some take this as liberating, even for Christian endeavors. I take it to be very bad news—philosophically, ethically, apologetically and theologically.

—DOUGLAS GROOTHUIS

Contents

Tables and Charts | viii

Foreword by Diane M. Wiater | ix

Preface | xi

Acknowledgements | xiii

Introduction | xv

Chapter 1: A Leader's Primer on Postmodernity | 1

Chapter 2: Answering Pilate's Inquiry, "What is Truth?" | 13

Chapter 3: Puritanical Leadership: A Commitment to Conscience | 25

Chapter 4: Vocational Leadership: A Sacred Calling | 37

Chapter 5: Leading by Loving: The Agape Supremacy | 50

Chapter 6: Reformational Leadership: Serving through the Solas | 62

Chapter 7: Leading Change in a Culture of Fluidity | 81

Chapter 8: Four C's of Christocentric Leadership: Courage, Credibility, Character, and Compassion | 96

Chapter 9: Servanthood: The Nemesis of Postmodernity | 110

Chapter 10: Communicating with Clarity in an Era of Fluidity | 126

Chapter 11: Epilogue | 141

Bibliography | 145

Tables and Charts

Table 1: Modern Versus Postmodern Principles of Management

Figure 1: Forty-Four Preferences of a Postmodern

Figure 2: A Force for Change: How Leadership Differs from Management

Figure 3: Compassionate Love and Servant Leadership, Conceptual Model

Figure 4: Types of Leadership Communicators

Foreword

If you've picked up this book because of the title, it is likely for you. As one peruses the ubiquitous works on leadership, it can be overwhelming to decide which are worth one's time and expense. Considering the vast array of sentiments on this topic, Liebhauser has chosen a path of substance based on something much more tangible than personal anecdotes, opinions, or even experiences. Rather, he uses illustrations from Christ and his followers through the ages to help the leader lead with confidence, conviction, and courage during this current age of chaos and confusion called "postmodernity."

In recent decades, leadership and everything about it has taken a center stage in common language and practice. Almost anyone can tell you that "everything rises and falls on leadership," but this is often the line used when leaders are failing or seemingly absent. Many people talk about leadership development, servant leadership, and transformational leadership. Some want to be better leaders, and many wish their leaders were better at leading. Yet with all the talk and knowledge concerning leadership, we still have many questions about leader competency and what it takes to be a good leader. This is even more pertinent when we talk about being a Christian leader.

We are in an era where we are accustomed to getting our questions answered as soon as we ask them. Siri®, Alexa®, and Google® are ready with a quick reply when we ask where the closest gas station or coffee shop is. We barely consider the response as we follow the directions provided.

Who is answering the questions about leadership, leader development, and Christ-centered leadership? Who is answering the culture question for us: how did we get here? Liebhauser meticulously exposes the biblical and scholarly origins of thought, while showing how these views are connected to Christian concepts and attempt to overtake them, so that there is only a shadow of biblical truth remaining in the mix. Liebhauser takes time to

Foreword

dissect what we know about leadership, particularly biblical or Christ-centered leadership. Finally, Liebhauser constructs a path with clear structure and markers, explaining why the shadow is not all it's cracked up to be and suggesting what is needed for Christian leadership.

As if the masterful depiction of deconstruction wasn't its own treat, it is Liebhauser's reconstruction that is most powerful and applicable to the reader. This thing called Christian leadership is far beyond memorizing some Scriptures; it goes deep into knowing Christ while being renewed by the word of God. *The Leadership Imperative* is a transformative read. The compression of truth is rich, filling, overwhelming, freeing, and challenging.

Why invest yourself in this read? Frankly, as a scholar, thought leader, reformer, cultural change agent, anthropologist, or a leader longing for deep and sure understanding and a foundation of leadership, you can't afford to bypass it. If you are expecting to do or become any of the above, you need to understand the elements of deconstruction and reconstruction of truth as presented in this work. Liebhauser takes the reader through "A Commitment to Conscience"; "Vocational Leadership: A Sacred Calling"; "Leading by Loving: The Agape Supremacy"; "Reformational Leadership: Serving through the Solas"; and "Leading Change in Culture of Fluidity." "The Four C's of Christocentric Leadership: Courage, Credibility, Character, and Compassion" is a logical, powerful, and anoited outcome of the previous chapters, which prepares leaders to lead boldly for God's glory. My favorite chapter is chapter 4, "Vocational Leadership: A Sacred Calling." The message in this chapter is clear, as Liebhauser notes: "Accordingly, Christian leaders are wise to ensure the utmost integrity in their labors, setting an example for others to follow." The lesson for leaders is to never elevate one type of work over another in an organization, even though their responsibilities and pay structures may differ. Each person should be treated with great respect, and all work accomplished with honesty, vigor, and verve should be honored.

Enough from me. I fully expect you'll find the depth of research, truth, and insight Liebhauser presents to be fulfilling, while at the same time find yourself intellectually and spiritually yearning for more.

Diane M. Wiater, PhD
CEO, Wiater Consulting Group
Professor, Regent University School of Business and Leadership

Preface

WITH A GENUINE CONCERN for the deficiency in courageous Christian leaders willing to proclaim the "whole counsel of God" (Acts 20:27) in this current postmodern era of dysfunction, ambiguity, and disorder, I embarked on this particular leadership theme. This work is designed to educate Christian leaders regarding the current era and its nuances and challenges, as well as provide encouragement through biblical solutions to lead faithfully, even counter-culturally, in these times. The postmodern age is designed to challenge (resist) authority, deconstruct language, and remove or redefine "truth" in rebellion against the empiricism of the modern era. This movement has created high hurdles for Christian leaders in their vocations, communities, and even their churches, as they seek to hold fast to an immutable God and His unchanging nature. Christian leaders can be encouraged that the narratives, indicatives, and imperatives of Scripture are equally as formidable today as in the time of their scribing. Although times may change, societal mores may crumble, and people may wander aimlessly, seeking truth, the message of the gospel is the same and does not require "candy coating" to reach people in this epoch. Leaders should emulate the Apostle Paul's approach,

> And I, when I came to you, brothers, did not come proclaiming to you the testimony of God with lofty speech or wisdom. For I decided to know nothing among you except Jesus Christ and him crucified. And I was with you in weakness and in fear and much trembling, and my speech and my message were not in plausible words of wisdom, but in demonstration of the Spirit and of power, so that your faith might not rest in the wisdom of men but in the power of God. (1 Cor 2:1–5[1])

1. All Biblical references throughout this book are derived from the English Standard Version (ESV) unless otherwise noted.

Preface

Paul did not seek the latest leadership guru's advice on how best to market the gospel, persuade people through emotional tactics, or water down the message to make it palatable. Instead, in humility, faith, and by God's wisdom through the Spirit, he effectively reached thousands of souls throughout his ministry. Biblical servanthood is the key to any God-honoring leadership theory.

Acknowledgements

I would like to gratefully acknowledge the enthusiastic support of my Professor and Project Chair, Dr. Diane Wiater, both throughout my doctoral journey and, specifically, during this work. Her advice, guidance, and prayers are deeply appreciated. Additionally, I wish to express my gratitude to Dr. Kathleen Patterson, Dr. Gary Oster, Dr. Doris Gomez, Dr. Russell Huizing, Dr. Virginia Richardson, Dr. Hadley Mitchell, Dr. David Stehlik, Col. (Ret.) David Augustine, Col. (Ret.) Rodger Seidel, Mr. Richard Daniels, and Mr. Frank Bartoe for their wise instruction and counsel which guided my thoughts while preparing this manuscript. Finally, I would like to recognize my parents, David and Carol Liebhauser, who have always supported my efforts. Thank you!

Introduction

IN THE CURRENT AGE of chaos, confusion, and ever-shifting cultural mores, Christian leaders have the daunting responsibility of presenting objective truth to a society basking in the muddy waters of postmodern ambiguity. This work presents the definitions, acrimony, nuances, challenges, and advantages of postmodernity, while encouraging and preparing Christian leaders to effectively and fruitfully lead amid an antithetical culture. In addition to dissecting postmodernity, this writing will cover leadership topics such as truth, conscience, vocation, *agape* love, leading through reformation principles, leading through change, leadership characteristics, servant leadership, and communication.

While postmodernity is difficult to define, the common thread involves a disconnection from anything empirical, historical, and authoritative. As each of these elements are consistent with biblical Christianity, Christian leaders today are challenged with leading in both secular and religious environments, due to losing the connection of previously established norms. The postmodern era is a result of the failures of the modern era, in its heavy emphasis on scientific inquiry, to fix all the world's woes. As a result, the pendulum of change has swung significantly, from a time where truth could only be discovered in a lab, to postmodernity, where each person determines his own truth without the need of a rational basis. Each of these eons presents hazards in engaging biblical truth.

In modern times, one would accept the premise that a man named Jesus Christ walked the earth over two thousand years ago due to the overwhelming historical evidence. In the postmodern age, however, people may discount the existence of Christ simply because of the way they feel. Furthermore, after discounting the life of Christ, the postmodern may take the liberty of developing his own "christ" and create his personal narrative of this god of his own device. Consequently, Christian leaders, although tempted to acquiesce to the postmodern intellectual gymnastics, must hold firm to the objective truth as presented in the Holy Scriptures.

1

A Leader's Primer on Postmodernity

So justice is driven back, and righteousness stands at a distance; truth has stumbled in the streets, honesty cannot enter. Truth is nowhere to be found, and whoever shuns evil becomes a prey.

—ISAIAH 59:14-15 (NIV)

THROUGHOUT AVIATION HISTORY, a multitude of fatal accidents have been determined to be caused by something known as "spatial disorientation." Spatial disorientation occurs when a pilot's brain is telling him something drastically different from his flight instrument panel. In this dilemma, the situation cannot be ignored, as the pilot must choose to rely on either his mind (feelings or rationale) or the airplane's navigation system. Such was the case with the 2000 crash of John F. Kennedy Jr.'s plane which claimed his life in addition to those of his wife Carolyn and her sister Lauren.[1] After the crash investigation had culminated, The New York Times reported, "Mr. Kennedy, who had not yet qualified for flying with instruments alone (as opposed to seeing visual cues through the windows), probably had less than one hour's experience flying his plane at night without an instructor."[2] The report noted that a common cause of crashes among pilots untrained in instrument flying was taking off when visibility was good (a situation

1. Tribune, "Disorientation," para 1.
2. Wald, "Safety Board," para 3.

known as Visual Flight Rules, or VFR) but flying into conditions where it was not, making the piloting more difficult than they can handle. In this case, the report said, the condition was hazy, which obscured the horizon. Pilots who cannot see the horizon must rely on instruments to tell if they are in level flight or if they are banking. A disoriented pilot can bank a plane into a fatal spiral.[3] One might ask at this point how spatial disorientation, JFK Jr., and a discussion on postmodernity are connected. Before this linkage transpires, it is important to present a universally accepted basis for postmodernism. As a renowned expert on postmodernity, Walter Truett Anderson posits,

> Postmodernity challenges the view that the truth is—as Isaiah Berlin put it—one and undivided, the same for all men everywhere at all times. The newer view regards any truth as socially constructed, contingent, inseparable from the peculiar needs and preferences of certain people in a certain time and place. This notion has many implications—it leaves no value, custom, belief, or eternal verity totally untouched.[4]

Based on this explanation of postmodernism, objective or absolute truth has been abrogated in this current era and substituted with a multitude of potentially contradicting truths which each person or group can determine for themselves.

Postmodern philosophy, therefore, creates the conundrum where each person bases decisions not on objective reality, but instead on feelings, emotions, experiences, and opinions of others, with the ability to change direction for any apparent reason. In the case of the crash of JFK Jr.'s airplane, several foreseeable components led to the disaster. First, a capable associate certified in instrumentation offered to pilot the aircraft on the date of flight, but was rejected. Second, the weather forecast presented challenges for a pilot only trained on visual flight rules (VFR). Third, due to the lack of confidence in the instrumentation, JFK Jr. relied on his instincts and best feelings at the time. Three objective options were available, which may have kept the three souls on board alive that fateful day. However, JFK Jr. rejected objective options and chose a path of no return.

Postmodernism parallels this tragic scenario. People who embrace its core tenets of relativism and subjectivism are left with nothing more than feelings, experience, and emotions to get through life. Determining right

---

3. Ibid, para 3.
4. Anderson, *The Future*, 27.

A Leader's Primer on Postmodernity

from wrong or wisdom from foolishness is based on the sources of our understanding and origin of truth. The book of Proverbs, considered part of the Bible's "wisdom literature," provides some pithy verses relating to trusting in oneself over objective truth,

- Whoever trusts in his own mind is a fool, but he who walks in wisdom will be delivered.[5]
- There is a way that seems right to a man, but its end is the way to death.[6]
- The way of a fool is right in his own eyes, but a wise man listens to advice.[7]

Postmodernism is like the pilot with access to the finest and most accurate technological instrumentation (objective truth) who chooses instead to rely on his faulty instincts (subjective truth). This mindset has taken hold of contemporary culture by influencing career choices, education, politics, art, moral and ethical decisions, and, most importantly, relationships—both with God and man. One's worldview determines how truth is understood, and its implications are significant. According to Doug Groothuis:

> The word "truth" is a staple in our language and in every language. One cannot imagine a human language lacking the concept of truth. Such a language would never inform anyone of anything: it would lack any intellectual access to reality. No language could be so constrained (although some political and celebrity "discourse" comes close). The idea of truth is part of the intellectual oxygen that we breathe. Whenever we state an opinion, defend, or critique an argument, ask a question, or investigate one kind of assertion or another, we presuppose the concept of truth—even if we do not directly state the word, even if we deny that truth is real or knowable.[8]

Consequently, when truth is relegated to opinion status, entire cultures enter into disorder.

Imagine a world where engineers use best guesses and assumptions in designing bridges, cars, and airplanes. The results of this process would be disastrous and chaotic. Fortunately, postmodernism has yet to fully deconstruct

5. Prov 28:26.
6. Prov 14:12.
7. Prov 12:15.
8. Groothuis, "Why Truth Matters," 441–54.

factual principles in the academic arenas of science, technology, engineering, and mathematics as it has in the realm of religion, ethics, and morality. Some might believe that creating doubt in the realm of belief will benefit society, as was popular in modernity. Unfortunately, moral frameworks and beliefs also provide a foundation for systems of law and order, and once they are dismantled, a culture of ambiguity, lawlessness, immorality, and distrust are perpetuated. This is the current situation in the United States, where accepted moral and ethical norms of the past have become questioned, mocked, and replaced by an individualized approach where each person creates his own version of truth. Just as a monetary system functions best with something akin to a gold standard, or a way to provide something substantive as a basis, laws also must have a foundation in a guiding principle. The founding fathers in America utilized a Judeo-Christian moral ethic in devising a system of law and order. Therefore, when a person commits an act of murder or thievery, it is not up to the police officer's version of right and wrong to decide to arrest the perpetrator; it is based on The Mosaic Law found in the Old Testament. In postmodern thought, the veracity of the Scriptures is to be questioned and summarily dismantled, as they are deemed too restrictive to open and free thinking and considered overly authoritarian. Just as the dollar loses its power when the backing authority is removed, so goes a well-functioning society when the basis of law is denigrated.

Although this work is not intended to enter the deeply philosophical nature of postmodernity, a brief synopsis of the eras will benefit the reader. While many scholars have chosen to label the eras of world history with different terminology, for the purposes of this writing, three epochs will be considered. The two eras preceding the current postmodern period are comprised of the premodern era and the modern era. Psychologist Dr. Louis Hoffman provides the following overview to understand the three primary eras based on epistemology and authority.

Premodernism (beginnings to 1650s)

Epistemology

The primary epistemology of the premodern period was based upon revealed knowledge from authoritative sources. In premodern times, it was believed that ultimate truth could be known and the way to this knowledge is through direct revelation. This direct revelation was generally assumed to come from God or a god.

Sources of Authority

The church, being the holder and interpreter of revealed knowledge, was the primary authority source in premodern times.

Modernism (1650s to 1950s)

Epistemology

Two new approaches to knowing became dominant in the modern period. The first was empiricism (knowing through the senses) which gradually evolved into scientific empiricism or modern science with the development of modernist methodology. The second epistemological approach of this period was reason or logic. Often, science and reason work collaboratively or in conjunction with each other.

Sources of Authority

As the shift in power moved away from the church, politics (governments, kings, etc.) and universities (scholars, professors) took over as the primary sources of authority. Oftentimes, a religious perspective was integrated into these modern authority sources, but the church no longer enjoyed the privileged power position.

Postmodernism (1950s to current times)

Epistemology

Postmodernism brought with it a questioning of the previous approaches to knowing. Instead of relying on one approach to knowing, they advocate for an epistemological pluralism, which utilizes multiple ways of knowing. This can include the premodern ways (revelation) and modern ways (science and reason), along with many other ways of knowing, such as intuition, relational, and spiritual.

Sources of Authority

Postmodern approaches seek to deconstruct previous authority sources and power. Because power is distrusted, they attempt to set up a less hierarchical approach, in which authority sources are more diffuse.[9]

A pattern which emerges from these three eras digresses from a focus and reverence for a strongly hierarchical construct to one which resents the notion of authority. The modern era appears to be a transition time between the two extremes, where scientific inquiry reigned supreme, even to the point of diminishing the need for God. Postmodernity, however, travels well beyond the empiricism of modernity into a realm of confusion, chaos, and pluralism, leaving each to discover his own truth. Grenz notes that "postmodern truth is relative to the community in which a person participates. And since there are many human communities, there are necessarily many different truths . . . As a result, postmodern relativistic pluralism seeks to give place to the 'local' nature of truth. Beliefs are held to be true within the context of the communities that espouse them."[10] Subsequently, even the smallest of subsets could determine their own aspect of truth apart from the community next door, impacting laws, commerce, and political structures.

The transition from the modern to the postmodern era was a result of discontentment with the authoritative aspect of science, for the former era limited the individual's right to choose. The postmodern era, however, allowed each person to become a god in the sense of determining truth. As White writes:

> In the eyes of postmoderns, then, modernism has failed, both as a prediction of progress and as a moral framework for culture. Thus, postmoderns take distinctly anti-modern views on the deeper questions of human life: social, political, moral, and spiritual questions. The failure of modernism means that there is no universal agreement and no prospect of universal agreement on these questions.[11]

To capture the prevailing mindset of postmodern thought, Isaías Díez del Río provides forty-four preferences of a postmodern:

---

9. Hoffman, "Premodernism, Modernism, & Postmodernism."
10. Grenz, *A Primer on Postmodernism*, 14–15.
11. White, *Postmodernism 101*, 45–46.

A Leader's Primer on Postmodernity

1. The individual to the universal
2. The psychological to the ideological
3. Communication to communion
4. Information to knowledge (truth)
5. Diversity to homogeneity
6. Permissiveness to coercion
7. Multi-criteria to norms and dogma
8. An eclectic approach to a systematic one
9. What is vital and existential to what is logical and reasonable
10. Opinion to ideas and thought
11. Sentiments to reason
12. Artisanship to art
13. Aesthetics to ethics
14. Syncretism to unity of belief
15. Multiculturalism to culture
16. Complete irrationalism to absolute rationalism
17. What is particular to what is universal or cosmopolitan
18. What is private and personal to what is public and social
19. Egoism to solidarity
20. Subjectivity to objectivity
21. Personal impulses and instinctual feelings to objective norms and values
22. Pleasure to asceticism and violence
23. Options to obligations
24. Frankness to secrecy
25. Human needs to technological demands
26. Multiplicity and difference to uniqueness and uniformity
27. Micro to macro
28. Minorities to majorities
29. Local/concrete contexts to global contexts
30. Marginal dissent to global consensus
31. Micro-groups to macro-communities
32. Emotional, sectarian communities to ecclesial communities
33. Spontaneous leaders to legal or traditional leaders
34. Personalism to authority
35. "Deconstruction" of the inherited world to its affirmation
36. "Decolonization" to colonization
37. The people, and ethnic groups, to the nation
38. Adolescent immaturity to adult maturity
39. Ambiguity to clarity and distinction
40. What is weak to what is strong
41. What is frivolous to what is serious
42. What is ephemeral, unstable, and transitory, to what is firm, stable, and lasting
43. Leisure and partying to work
44. Consumerism to production[1]

Figure 1

The focus of postmodernity, more than anything else, is self. Self is the foundation of knowledge, truth, wisdom, morality, ethics, and reality. The challenge with this equation is that unity and cohesion toward a common goal are seemingly elusive as each person pursues his own direction. Phillips and Okholm consider desire, a primary element of self-interest, as integral:

> In American postmodernism, the moral and metaphysical foundations of Romanticism simply drop away, leaving the self driven by the single engine of desire. Postmodernism in America is Romanticism stripped of its pretensions. Marx, Nietzsche, and Freud materialized and demystified the transcendent self celebrated in the Enlightenment and Romanticism . . . All that language can reveal, the postmodern argument concludes from its loss of Romantic faith, are the self's desires—desires for sexual gratification, economic gain, pleasure, and power.[12]

12. Phillips and Okholm, *Christian*, 27.

The Leadership Imperative

In a very real sense, people today are scattered in a similar way to God's punishment of Babel, as illustrated in the Genesis pericope:

> "Come, let us go down and there confuse their language, so that they may not understand one another's speech." So, the Lord dispersed them from there over the face of all the earth, and they left off building the city. Therefore, its name was called Babel, because there the Lord confused the language of all the earth. And from there the Lord dispersed them over the face of all the earth.[13]

Regarding this correlation, Veith comments:

> This is exactly what happened with the fall of modernism. The monolithic sensibility of modernism, which seemed to have an unlimited potential, has fragmented into diverse and competing communities. People can no longer understand each other. There are no common reference points, no common language. Totalitarian unity has given way to chaotic diversity. Scattered in small groups of like-minded people, those who speak the same language, human beings today are confused.[14]

God reversed the curse of Abel in a remarkable way at Pentecost, as exemplified in the Acts 2 narrative:

> When the day of Pentecost arrived, they were all together in one place. And suddenly there came from heaven a sound like a mighty rushing wind, and it filled the entire house where they were sitting. And divided tongues as of fire appeared to them and rested on each one of them. And they were all filled with the Holy Spirit and began to speak in other tongues as the Spirit gave them utterance. Now there were dwelling in Jerusalem Jews, devout men from every nation under heaven. And at this sound the multitude came together, and they were bewildered, because each one was hearing them speak in his own language. And they were amazed and astonished, saying, "Are not all these who are speaking Galileans? And how is it that we hear, each of us in his own native language? Parthians and Medes and Elamites and residents of Mesopotamia, Judea and Cappadocia, Pontus and Asia, Phrygia and Pamphylia, Egypt and the parts of Libya belonging to Cyrene, and visitors from Rome, both Jews and proselytes, Cretans and Arabians—we hear them telling in

---

13. Gen 11:7–9.
14. Veith, *Postmodern Times*, 21.

our own tongues the mighty works of God." And all were amazed and perplexed, saying to one another, "What does this mean?"[15]

This selection presents the reader with the prospect of unity which is only found in Christ. While the rest of the world continues its confused Babel-like course, God has provided, through the gospel of Jesus Christ, the opportunity for faith, coherency, consistency, objectivity, peace, and purpose on his terms, not man's. Veith writes, "Because of this larger perspective, God's people will see the futility of both the building of the Tower and the cacophony of voices which followed its abandonment. They will likewise recognize the limitations of both the modernists and the postmodernists. Once again, the issue will be sin, idolatry, and language."[16]

This work seeks to present the current state of the world under the moniker of "postmodernism" as a system filled with peril, haziness, and bedlam while providing a framework of hope for the Christian leader. The premodern, modern, and postmodern eras all failed at elevating God and found unique paths to place man at the center of the universe. The premodern era placed "truth" squarely in the hands of a small group of educated Roman Catholic clergy to feed the masses. Unfortunately, humanity does not handle the prospect of power well, for it eventually lords it over others instead of seeking ways to serve them. Eventually, distrust of the clergy led to the desire for empirical evidence to provide a basis for truth. The modern era provided this and used science as its tool, not to honor God as the source of all knowledge, but instead to relegate him to a historical footnote. As the science lab could not prove the existence of God, he could not exist. Next, scientific evidence was not robust enough to convince people in regard to truth. They did not want the educated nor the clergy telling them what they must believe, so the postmodern era began and continues. Veith posits:

> Today we see the rejection of all foundations. The various projects of modernism involved destroying foundations and replacing them with foundations of a different kind. Today, the modern has become obsolete, and the futility of this never-ending cycle of demolition and reconstruction has become evident. The postmodernists pose an entirely different alternative. Perhaps we can build without foundations.[17]

---

15. Acts 2:1–12.
16. Veith, *Postmodern Times*, 23.
17. Ibid., 225.

The Leadership Imperative

The idea of "foundations" is based on the Biblical house/foundation metaphor as used by Christ to illustrate the notion of wisdom. According to Matthew's gospel,

> Everyone then who hears these words of mine and does them will be like a wise man who built his house on the rock. And the rain fell, and the floods came, and the winds blew and beat on that house, but it did not fall, because it had been founded on the rock. And everyone who hears these words of mine and does not do them will be like a foolish man who built his house on the sand. And the rain fell, and the floods came, and the winds blew and beat against that house, and it fell, and great was the fall of it.[18]

The postmodern foundation is Christless, purposeless, aimless, and fruitless. Therefore, Christian leaders must become aware of the prevailing culture and be equipped to lead faithfully by presenting veracity to a truth-deprived people.

The task of today's Christian leader is to boldly present truth in an age of uncertainty with humility, courage, love, compassion, conviction, and grace. University of Chicago Professor Martin Marty paints a dire picture of postmodernity in its understanding of truth,

> What is truth? Truth is the zone in which decisions about gods and lords, God and Lord, are made and grow complex. Almost all students, victims, or advertisers of postmodernity notice that relativity and relativism are characteristic features of whatever it is. In premodern situations, there was one privileged channel of truth. Absolutes came from the laws, legends, and customs handed down by seniors or other authorities. Modernity presented a circumstance where there were many truths, but some principled use of reason aided in discriminating and coming through critical inquiry to truth. In postmodernity, relativism at worst and relativity at best complicate the seeker of a way, The Way. As one teacher reported, a student wrote, "Hitler had his ideas and way of life, and I have mine. How do I get to judge what he lived by?" This is the extreme case that prepares us for all the moderate ones along the way.[19]

Marty's quote reveals the battle for objectivity in an age of ambiguity. The ensuing chapters will seek to equip leaders by preparing their hearts and minds to successfully lead in a countercultural pursuit and to present truth

---

18. Matt 7:24–27.
19. Marty, "Youth," 33.

to those who believe that they already have truth. This task is exceptionally challenging, as paradigms must be shattered, hearts must be broken, and lives must be changed. Through the flesh, this commission is impossible, but by the Holy Spirit working through the believing leader, all things are possible (Mark 9:23).

Although the task of preparing the Christian leader living in postmodern times seems daunting, every era of human history has sought to undermine absolute truth. As Solomon wrote, "What has been will be again, what has been done will be done again; there is nothing new under the sun."[20] While the mechanism of attack against truth today may be dissimilar, the response has remained unchanged. The same Scriptures used by Christ, the Apostles, and countless martyrs through the ages, is just as powerful today is it was when inscribed. The Christian leader must not fear these postmodern times, but should instead embrace them with verve, knowing that absolute truth will ultimately prevail. Christian leaders need not devise new tactics to allure the masses to truth; rather, they should embrace the simplicity of the Apostle Paul's approach. He proclaimed:

> And I, when I came to you, brothers, did not come proclaiming to you the testimony of God with lofty speech or wisdom. For I decided to know nothing among you except Jesus Christ and him crucified. And I was with you in weakness and in fear and much trembling, and my speech and my message were not in plausible words of wisdom, but in demonstration of the Spirit and of power, so that your faith might not rest in the wisdom of men but in the power of God.[21]

If Paul lacked the need for cleverness in reaching the masses, the Christian leader will do well to follow suit. In his work *Postmodernism 101*, Heath White encapsulates well the Christian's focus in postmodernity:

> The tides of human culture have always been as changeable as the sea—placid at times, stormy at others. The present transition to postmodernism is on the stormy side. The Bible, however, gives us images of God as "the Rock eternal," and of the gospel as "an anchor for the soul, firm and secure." Although the way God reveals himself and his message to each generation may differ, God himself does not change, nor does the good news he offers us in Jesus Christ. In this new time of our culture, with new threats and new challenges

---

20. Eccl 1:9 (NIV).
21. 1 Cor 2:1–10.

and new opportunities, God's promises remain secure. That is the most important knowledge to carry into the postmodern world.[22]

While many view this era with hopelessness and fear, the Christian leader has the ability to stand firm in truth and be an example of God's unchanging love and grace during a time of transforming ideas of love and selfishness. The best and most effective apologetic available to the Christian leader is *truth* as exclusively provided in God's holy word.

---

22. White, *Postmodernism 101*, 164.

2

Answering Pilate's Inquiry, "What is Truth?"

> *There is something missing in my life, and it has to do with my need to understand what I must do, not what I must know—except, of course, that a certain amount of knowledge is presupposed in every action. I need to understand my purpose in life, to see what God wants me to do, and this means that I must find a truth which is true for me, that I must find that idea for which I can live and die.*
>
> —SØREN KIERKEGAARD[1]

IN THE ABOVE QUOTE, well-known philosopher Søren Kierkegaard presents his struggle as a university student with the concept of truth and God's purpose in his life in relation to that truth. A subtle phrase in this quote, "and this means that I must find a truth which is true for me," provides a suitable starting point in any discussion of postmodernism or postmodernity. Kierkegaard was not seeking "the truth"; instead, he was seeking something much different: his own truth. Although this point may seem trivial, the drift from objective to subjective truth on a societal scale revolutionizes not only philosophical thinking, but also how people act and live in a culture where each person creates his own truth. In the famous dialogue between Jesus Christ and the Roman prefect, Pontius Pilate, the element of objective truth

---

1. Groothius, *Truth Decay*, 10.

was on trial as Pilate had the authority to free the innocent Christ because he had found "no guilt in him."[2] Consider the following discourse:

> So Pilate entered his headquarters again and called Jesus and said to him, "Are you the King of the Jews?" Jesus answered, "Do you say this of your own accord, or did others say it to you about me?" Pilate answered, "Am I a Jew? Your own nation and the chief priests have delivered you over to me. What have you done?" Jesus answered, "My kingdom is not of this world. If my kingdom were of this world, my servants would have been fighting, that I might not be delivered over to the Jews. But my kingdom is not from the world." Then Pilate said to him, "So you are a king?" Jesus answered, "You say that I am a king. For this purpose I was born and for this purpose I have come into the world—to bear witness to the truth. Everyone who is of the truth listens to my voice." Pilate said to him, "What is truth?"[3]

As Pilate struggled with the concept of truth, he decided to allow the Jewish people to usurp his authority and release a criminal, thus sending the sinless Christ to an excruciating execution on the cross of Calvary. Hence, one's view of truth can have severe consequences, even leading to death. An untold number of Christian martyrs have since been murdered for their unwillingness to deny truth. How one deals with the element of truth will dictate the course of life just as one hiking in a foreign area may choose to follow his compass into safety or his feelings into a dangerous place. The compass metaphor is beneficial because it illustrates objectivity based on magnetism: "True north" is the same direction, no matter where the starting point may be. Along similar lines, objective truth does not change, regardless of the country, the culture, the time, or the people.

Pilate, just as those in positions of leadership today, had a moral obligation to oversee the trial of Christ by considering the objective evidence and ruling accordingly. It is evident in this passage that Pilate found that Christ did not break any laws and that the allegations against him were baseless. However, Pilate was more concerned with his own power and livelihood than leading the people according to truth. Groothuis writes,

> When Pontius Pilate interrogated Jesus before His crucifixion, Jesus proclaimed, "Everyone on the side of truth listens to me." (John 18:37). To this Pilate replied, "What is truth?" and immediately left Jesus to address the Jews who wanted Christ crucified

---

2. John 18:38.
3. John 18:33–38.

Answering Pilate's Inquiry, "What is Truth?"

(v. 38). As philosopher Francis Bacon wrote, "What is truth?" said jesting Pilate; and would not stay for an answer. Although we have no record of any reply by Jesus, Christians affirm that Pilate was staring Truth in the face, for Jesus had stated earlier to Thomas, "I am the way and the truth and the life." (John 14:6)[4]

Groothuis's point parallels each person's decision to determine the nature of truth, even when it is looking him in the eyes. Accordingly, when faced with the truth of the gospel of Christ, each person may either accept the reality of the claim, or, as Pilate, shrug it off and walk away. Unfortunately, the consequences of ignoring truth bring temporal and eternal ramifications.

Leading in postmodernity presents a host of challenges, as historically accepted truths are defied and yesterday's taboos become legal, accepted, and promoted. Evangelical theologian Carl F. H. Henry presents this dilemma:

> Few times in history has revealed religion been forced to contend with such serious problems of truth and word, and never in the past have the role of words and the nature of truth been as misty and undefined as now. Only if we recognize that the truth of truth . . . is today in doubt, and that this uncertainty stifles the word as a carrier of God's truth and moral judgment, do we fathom the depth of the current crisis. When the truth and word remain as the accepted universe of discourse, then all aberrations can be challenged in the name of truth. Today, however, the nature of truth and even the role of words is in dispute.[5]

Christian leaders who hold to the inerrancy of Scripture must find a way to lead without compromise in a world found to be skeptical, critical, and increasingly antagonistic to absolute truth. The postmodern era presents severe hurdles to faithful leadership, but this work will reveal that "What has been is what will be, and what has been done is what will be done, and there is nothing new under the sun."[6] Consequently, although the prevailing winds are pushing against truth, the Christian leader need not fear. In fact, it may be that in these times of ambiguity, truth may be a welcome prospect for many.

As truth is a pervasive term, it is important for Christian leaders to have a working knowledge of truth to live it out and present it to others. As MacArthur writes:

---

4. Groothius, *Truth Decay*, 23.
5. Henry, *God, Revelation, and Authority*, 24.
6. Eccl 1:9.

The Leadership Imperative

> Of course, God and truth are inseparable. Every thought about the essence of truth—what it is, what makes it "true," and how we can possibly know anything for sure, quickly moves us back to God. That is why God incarnate—Jesus Christ—is called the truth (John 14:6). That is why it is not particularly surprising when someone who repudiates God rejects His truth as well. If a person can't tolerate the thought of God, there is simply no comfortable place for the concept of truth in that person's worldview, either. So the consistent atheist, agnostic, or idolater might as well hate the very idea of truth. After all, to reject God is to reject the Giver of all truth, the final Judge of what really is true, and the very essence and embodiment of truth itself.[7]

Consequently, objective truth begins and ends with God himself. Truth in postmodern times becomes like polytheism in other religions where a multitude of gods exists for various purposes. As each person develops his own form of truth, he is essentially acting as a god by being the source of something beyond himself. This is a tragic and perilous course as the result is an utter decimation of decency and goodness. This results in broken homes, the destruction of traditional marriage, the termination of unborn children, and the devaluing of all human life.

For those working outside of objective truth, peace is unknowable as people are always in a state of flux, wondering what to do in each situation where no clear standard of right and wrong exists. The result of this worldview played out to its natural conclusion is selfism, hedonism, socialism, lawlessness, and even anarchy. A world without moral boundaries is a world without joy, peace, and prosperity. The only truth which can be a cause of blessing, protection, and goodness is the truth prescribed in God's written word and that which mirrors his attributes. Per Groothuis,

> God's truth is grounded in God's eternal being. It has no expiration date and needs no image makeovers. Moreover, it is a living, personal, and dynamic truth—a truth that transcends trivialities of our age and touches us at the deepest levels of our beings by including us in an eternal drama. This truth transforms us, as David knew well: "I have hidden your word in my heart that I might not sin against you" (Ps 119:11).[8]

The leader, therefore, must be connected to this truth in a most personal way; he must be part of the body of Christ, having trusted in and being a follower

---

7. MacArthur, *The Truth War*, 24.
8. Groothuis, *Truth Decay*, 74.

of the risen Savior. Pink notes, "The foundation of all true knowledge of God must be a clear mental apprehension of His perfections as revealed in Holy Scripture. An unknown God can neither be trusted, served, nor worshiped."[9]

As absolute truth is grounded in the Bible; the reading and studying of the Scriptures must be accomplished with the goal of seeking the author's (God's) intent. This methodology of scriptural exegesis is antithetical to postmodernism, as the postmodernist aims to read any text as one with fluid meaning in which he alone can dissect the truth. Part and parcel to postmodernism's deconstruction of truth is a redefinition of terms, even those universally accepted. For the postmodernist, a work of art, a novel, or even the Bible is to be defined by what the beholder sees and feels, completely disregarding the artist's or author's purpose. Betty Jean Craige, in *Reconnection: Dualism to Holism in Literary Study*, presents the postmodern view of language, meaning, and interpretation:

1. Things and events do not have intrinsic meaning. There is no inherent objectivity, only continuous interpretation of the world.
2. Continuous examination of the world requires a contextual examination of things. We are part of that context.
3. The interpretation of a text depends on the relative viewpoint and the particular values of the interpreter. To understand a text on the basis of one's life relation to it is to have preunderstanding. Interpretation does not depend on the external text nor its author.
4. Language is not neutral but is relative and is value-laden. It is the medium through which we do our thinking.
5. Language and discourse convey ideology, and a society's intellectual discourse rests on political values and affects society in political ways.[10]

Craige's capricious view of language and meaning may prevent the didactic element from being received from a text. Furthermore, this mindset will likely confuse the reader by placing the burden on him to create a clear understanding of the writing, void of the author's aim. Regarding the knowledge of Scripture, the reader must seek God's design for the passage if he wishes to benefit from its instruction. While mankind's tendency is to enjoy the comforting aspects of the Scripture (e.g., heaven, blessings, joy, peace, prosperity, wisdom, etc.) and shun, ignore, or disregard the bad news (e.g.,

---

9. Pink, *Attributes of God*, 5.
10. Craige, *Reconnection*, 204.

sin, hell, pain, suffering, etc.), both must be given equal authority for a true picture of the text to occur. Just as a car battery requires both a positive and a negative charge to function, so do those who seek the blessings of God through his word. Therefore, knowing the author will aid the reader in understanding his communication. Noebel writes,

> God chose to communicate the Truth about Himself and His world by words contained in the Scriptures and the language of the heavens (Ps 19). God's words do not depend upon a reader's interpretation. Instead, the reader is to interpret the Bible according to God's intention. The Apostle Peter is clear when he writes, "Above all, you must understand that no prophecy of Scripture came about by the prophet's own interpretation. For prophecy never had its origin in the will of man, but men spoke from God as they were carried along by the Holy Spirit" (2 Pet 1:19–21).[11]

Words have meaning. The goal of postmodernism is to allow each person to be his own Webster's Dictionary and change definitions at will. If one can successfully deconstruct universally agreed-upon terms and phrases, no one will have certainty about anything. So, life without a basis for meaning is one without purpose. Deconstructionism, therefore, affects every facet of culture and life as it attempts to blur the lines and increase indistinctness. In his book *The American Hour*, Os Guinness notes:

> Under postmodern conditions, words lose their authority and become accessory to images. The past is no longer a heritage, but a debris-strewn ruin to be ransacked for a bric-a-brac of beliefs that is as incoherent as it is inconsequential . . . The grand flirtation with the meaninglessness of modernity goes on, but in a party mood. Religion is no longer transcendent, but a recreational pursuit for the connoisseurs of "spirituality." Art, homes, lifestyles, ideas, character, self-renewal, and even belief in God all become auxiliary to sales and the ceaseless consumption of styles.[12]

Guinness connects the perceived meaninglessness of terminology to the shallowness of all other human endeavors when truth is set aside for fiction. If words with concrete meaning (truth) can be deconstructed, people will begin to question the reality of everything that exists. The late German philosopher and Christian antagonist Friedrich Wilhelm Nietzsche expressed his ideas regarding truth:

---

11. Noebel, *Understanding the Times*, 211.
12. Guiness, *The American Hour*, 129.

Answering Pilate's Inquiry, "What is Truth?"

> What, then, is truth? A mobile army of metaphors, metonyms, and anthropomorphisms—in short, a sum of human relations, which have been enhanced, transposed, and embellished poetically and rhetorically, and which after long use seem firm, canonical, and obligatory to a people: truths are illusions about which one has forgotten that this is what they are; metaphors which are worn out and without sensuous power, coins which have lost their pictures and now matter only as metal, no longer as coins.[13]

The absurdity of Nietzsche's statement is noteworthy in that it could never be accepted as true based on his own assertion that "truths are illusions." Many have sought to dismantle reality, but it appears to be a vain attempt due to its basis in contradiction and circular argumentation.

Consequently, evangelism for the Christian leader can be a daunting task. Prior-accepted considerations of history, logic, eyewitness accounts, and terminology are all sacrificed at the altar of pluralism, relativism, syncretism, and subjectivism. Even sharing accounts of a man named Jesus who walked the earth over two thousand years ago can be quickly discounted, regardless of the overwhelming evidence of its reality. When one can choose to ignore the historicity of Jesus Christ, the veracity of the resurrection and other miracles will bring only mockery and laughter by many. The Christian leader must take solace in the fact that only Christ can regenerate souls, even though Christians in postmodernity may struggle in presenting the gospel to myopic people. The Apostle Paul writes, "So neither he who plants nor he who waters is anything, but only God who gives the growth."[14] While Paul is not minimizing the importance and necessity of evangelism, he is making it clear that salvation belongs to God alone.

While each era in history found its way to discount, neglect, and reject God through ignorance and evil, God has always broken through to rescue his own (John 10:39, 17:2–24). In postmodernity, the great commission is the same as it was in the premodern and modern eras. What has changed is that the type of deception which captivates people's hearts and minds as truth is lost in logomachy, regardless of the argument's persuasiveness. Those living during the Old Testament period were just as recalcitrant to divine truth as twenty-first-century postmodernists. The prophet Isaiah proclaimed:

---

13. Nietzsche, *Truth and Extra-Moral Sense*, 46–47.
14. 1 Cor 3:7.

> And I heard the voice of the Lord saying, "Whom shall I send, and who will go for us?" Then I said, "Here am I! Send me." And he said, "Go, and say to this people: 'Keep on hearing, but do not understand; keep on seeing, but do not perceive.' Make the heart of this people dull, and their ears heavy, and blind their eyes; lest they see with their eyes, and hear with their ears, and understand with their hearts, and turn and be healed."[15]

As the Lord removed the blindness of countless men and women throughout time, his method has not changed regarding the *ordo salutis* (order of salvation). Therefore, although the contemporary Christian leader may grow frustrated in attempting to convince the postmodernist of objective truth, he must rely on the power of the Holy Spirit to change the minds of pedantic peoples.

The search for truth and wisdom has befuddled philosophers for thousands of years. As one who struggled with the concept of truth more openly than other philosophers, Aristotle stated: "To say of what is that it is not, or of what is not that it is, is false, while to say of what is that it is, and of what is not that it is not, is true; so that he who says of anything that it is, or that it is not, will say either what is true or what is false".[16] Truth, therefore, is not a matter of one's own interpretation or reality but is based on something objective and unchanging. Christian philosopher Nicholas Wolterstorff illustrates this idea, "If I believe of something that it is a duck, that is true of it if and only if it is a duck. And if that is indeed true of it, it is not true of it relative to some conceptual scheme. It is just true, period. Thoughts are true or false or things, period—not relative to something or other."[17] Truth, then, requires something unmovable, unchanging, and eternal to ground it permanently, which is only found in the God of creation.

As the only viable source of truth in written form, the holy Scriptures reveal the author of truth as the blessed Trinity to include the Father, Son, and Holy Spirit. For this reason, Christian leaders must become Bereans and study the word intently as,

> His divine power has granted to us all things that pertain to life and godliness, through the knowledge of him who called us to his own glory and excellence, by which he has granted to us his precious and very great promises, so that through them you may

---

15. Isa 6:8–10.
16. Aristotle, *Metaphysics* 4.7.
17. Groothius, *Truth Decay*, 88.

Answering Pilate's Inquiry, "What is Truth?"

become partakers of the divine nature, having escaped from the corruption that is in the world because of sinful desire.[18]

This pericope presents truth as divine "knowledge," rescuing those who believe. Accordingly, if truth is not based on fact, but instead on one's own judgment, the knowledge of saving grace is inaccessible, and the way of escape is shuttered. MacArthur writes:

> A biblical perspective of truth also necessarily entails the recognition that ultimate truth is an objective reality. Truth exists outside of us and remains the same regardless of how we may perceive it. Truth by definition is as fixed and constant as God is immutable. That is because real truth is the unchanged and unchanging expression of who God is; it is not our own personal and arbitrary interpretation of reality.[19]

The challenge to MacArthur's assertion that truth is not "our own personal and arbitrary interpretation of reality" is evident by postmodernists unwilling to see themselves as receivers, rather than creators of knowledge. The postmodernists cannot fathom someone outside of themselves being the ultimate source of truth. This reveals the goal of postmodernism to be quasi-polytheistic, where a multitude of gods exist and all in the form of man.

The effective Christian leader will be grounded in truth, in submission to the God of truth, and continually seeking truth via God's holy word. To present truth, one must know truth and its source. Jesus Christ presents himself as "truth," and the only path to divine knowledge, as he declares "I am the way, and the truth, and the life. No one comes to the Father except through me."[20] Jesus presented this exclusive claim of sovereignty as the only way to the Father, and his claim may either be rejected or accepted as truth. In his acclaimed work *Mere Christianity*, C. S. Lewis presents the truth claims about Christ as having three response options: liar, Lord, or lunatic,

> I am trying here to prevent anyone saying the really foolish thing that people often say about Him: "I'm ready to accept Jesus as a great moral teacher, but I don't accept his claim to be God." That is the one thing we must not say. A man who was merely a man and said the sort of things Jesus said would not be a great moral teacher. He would either be a lunatic—on the level with the man who says he is a poached egg—or else he would be the Devil of

---

18. 2 Pet 1:3–4.
19. MacArthur, *Truth War*, xx.
20. John 14:6.

> Hell. You must make your choice. Either this man was, and is, the Son of God, or else a madman or something worse. You can shut him up for a fool; you can spit at him and kill him as a demon or you can fall at his feet and call him Lord and God. But let us not come with any patronising nonsense about his being a great human teacher. He has not left that open to us. He did not intend to.[21]

Lewis discloses three options by which humanity may view Christ. Two of them are based on prevarication, and one is based on the *sine qua non*: Jesus Christ as Lord. If the truth of Jesus Christ is summarily rejected, it is hard to imagine any other truth being uncompromised and open to interpretation.

The truth of Christ cannot be merely known or even accepted, as "even the demons obey and shudder!"[22] Instead, the reality of a relationship with Christ must be lived out with integrity, humility, courage, and grace. The Christian leader must unashamedly follow Christ and present an example for others to follow to ensure that his talk and walk are aligned well. The observer may be fascinated with sound theology pulled straight from Scripture, but it may quickly be dismissed if the leader's words and actions are not symbiotic. The great nineteenth-century British preacher Charles Haddon Spurgeon asserted:

> If we would show decision for the truth, we must not only do so by our tone and manner but by our daily actions. A man's life is always more forcible than his speech; when men take stock of him, they reckon his deeds as pounds and his words as pence. If his life and his doctrines disagree, the mass of lookers-on accept his practice and reject his preaching. A man may know a great deal about truth, and yet be a very damaging witness on its behalf, because he is no credit to it.[23]

Truth, therefore, is the starting point and not the finishing line, as it is not enough to accept truth if one is not willing to live up to it.

As postmodernism struggles to understand the rudimentary elements of truth, the Christian leader must be willing and able to present it boldly without equivocation. MacArthur writes, "The current climate of postmodernism does represent a wonderful opportunity for the church of Jesus Christ. The arrogant rationalism that dominated the modern era is already in its death throes. Most of the world is caught up in disillusionment and

---

21. Lewis, *Mere Christianity*, 52.
22. Jas 2:19.
23. Spurgeon, "The Need," para. 17.

Answering Pilate's Inquiry, "What is Truth?"

confusion. People are unsure about virtually everything and do not know where to turn for truth."[24] In an age of muddle, a leader with a firm grip on reality, grounded in truth, will be a welcomed sight to many who are floundering in fluidity, unable to make moral decisions without even a modicum of confidence. The church, then, should be the beacon of hope and the anchor of stability where seekers can find answers to stand the test of time and eternity. Author and pastor Albert Mohler describes the transformation of truth through the ages:

> On the question of truth in contemporary culture, the postmodern age confronts the church with a challenge of several dimensions. First, a deconstruction of truth. Truth has always been a matter of contention. Throughout all the centuries, even as far back as the pre-Socratic philosophers, truth was the major issue of philosophical concern and inquiry. Postmodernism, however, has turned this concern for truth on its head. While most arguments throughout history have been disputes between rival claims to truth, postmodernism rejects the very notion of truth as a fixed universal, or objective absolute. Modernist thinkers had earlier rejected revelation as a source of truth and, confident that their approach would yield objective and universal truths by means of autonomous human reason, had attempted to establish truth on the basis of inductive thought and scientific investigation. Postmodernists reject both these approaches, arguing that neither revelation nor the scientific method is a reliable source for truth. According to postmodern theory, truth is not objective or absolute at all, nor can it be determined by any commonly accepted method. Instead, postmodernists argue that truth is socially constructed, plural, and inaccessible to universal reason, which itself does not exist anyway. As postmodern philosopher Richard Rorty asserts, "Truth is made rather than found."[25]

In Rorty's statement, "Truth is made rather than found," he is allowing for a system of complete pandemonium where a judge could free a mass-murderer based on his opinion that the defendant didn't "really mean to kill those people," or a professor could give his failing students top grades because "it will make them feel better about themselves."

Rorty's statement would be laughable if society were not so quickly embracing this mindset. While absurd and lacking in any logical basis, it

---

24. MacArthur, *The Truth War*, 24.
25. Mohler, "What is Truth?", 63–75.

is important for Christian leaders to understand the worldview of many in today's workforce as they will be charged with leading others to perform objective labors from a subjective worldview. In addition, the "deconstruction of truth" is playing out in the broader evangelical church with many people questioning and revising historic orthodoxy on matters of marriage, abortion, and social welfare. Through the analogy of faith, the Scriptures are abundant and clear on these and other matters. Even essential issues to the Christian faith, such as the resurrection of Christ, are being deconstructed, while the biblical and historical evidences are clear. According to Sarot:

> Historical criticism came up with an alternative view of the Resurrection. This alternative view may be summarised[sic] as follows: In accordance with Jewish beliefs about the resurrection of martyrs, Paul, the earliest writer of the New Testament, held the opinion that three days after his death, Jesus rose and ascended to heaven in a new, spiritual body. The idea of the empty grave is a legend, composed by Mark, the first Gospel writer. He interpreted the original story about a Resurrection in heaven in Greco-Roman terms as a Resurrection of the earthly body: Just like Hercules, Aeneas, and Romulus, Jesus ascended to heaven in his earthly body, leaving behind an empty grave.[26]

Although the Scriptures are clear that Jesus was carried to the tomb dead and exited alive, skeptics seek to dismantle this core tenant of Christianity and break the confidence of the faithful. Paul provides a warning against this heresy when he writes, "If Christ has not been raised, our preaching is useless and so is your faith. More than that, we are then found to be false witnesses about God, for we have testified about God that he raised Christ from the dead."[27] Paul understood that the destruction of the resurrection account meant that Christianity was a passing fallacy and should be summarily dismissed. Since the apostolic era, many have devised alternate theories in attempts to destroy the faith, but the postmodern era allows for the questioning of not merely the resurrection, but even the existence of a man named Jesus who walked the earth two thousand years ago. Thus, Christian leaders must remain committed to the inerrancy and sufficiency of Scripture lest they also become deceived and lead others astray.

---

26. Sarot, "The Ultimate Miracle?", 1–9.
27. 1 Cor 15:14–15 (NIV).

3

Puritanical Leadership

A Commitment to Conscience

> For all who have sinned without the law will also perish without the law, and all who have sinned under the law will be judged by the law. For it is not the hearers of the law who are righteous before God, but the doers of the law who will be justified. For when Gentiles, who do not have the law, by nature do what the law requires, they are a law to themselves, even though they do not have the law. They show that the work of the law is written on their hearts, while their conscience also bears witness, and their conflicting thoughts accuse or even excuse them on that day when, according to my gospel, God judges the secrets of men by Christ Jesus.[1]
>
> —ROMANS 2:12-16

LEADERS, ESPECIALLY THOSE WHO faithfully wear the Christian moniker, are under enormous pressure to both succeed and to fail. The Christian leader is constantly being observed to see how he might handle stress, temptation, insults, ethical conflicts, and times of pain and sorrow. Handling each of these with conviction, grace, and humility may garner high favor, but one small slip may prove disastrous to his reputation and witness for Christ. Therefore, Christian leaders must be ever careful to maintain a clear

---

1. Emphasis added.

conscience and live according to that which is good. This is no easy task, as life is full of unexpected hurdles and ubiquitous enticements. The probity of the Christian leader must remain intact if he is to both honor his God and to remain faithful in vocation. As a protection mechanism, God gave each person a conscience to send out warnings against sin. Although the conscience is fallible and cannot be considered the voice of God, it is an internal system created to caution the soul of impending danger. When the conscience is clean, it has the clarity of a well-functioning air traffic control computer, clearly displaying all the hazards in the air. If this computer glitches or crashes, the results could prove devastating. For this reason, air traffic control systems are continually monitored and upgraded to run at peak performance. In like manner, the conscience must be maintained through prayer, scriptural studies, and right living.

Baker's *Dictionary of Biblical Theology* defines the conscience as:

> A term that describes an aspect of a human being's self-awareness. It is part of a person's internal rational capacity and is not, as popular lore sometimes suggests, an audience room for the voice of God or of the devil. Conscience is a critical inner awareness that bears witness to the norms and values we recognize and apply. The complex of values with which conscience deals includes not only those we own but the entire range of values to which we are exposed during life's journey.[2]

Although the definition and foundation of the conscience have been disputed throughout the centuries, a common theme revolves around its ability to warn a person of something unwise or evil. When these warnings are continually disregarded, the conscience becomes defiled, and the person no longer seeks to honor God, but instead begins a course of destruction. Paul provided a vivid admonition to the church in Rome, regarding the defilement of conscience and its dire consequence:

> Therefore God gave them up in the lusts of their hearts to impurity, to the dishonoring of their bodies among themselves, because they exchanged the truth about God for a lie and worshiped and served the creature rather than the Creator, who is blessed forever! Amen. For this reason God gave them up to dishonorable passions. For their women exchanged natural relations for those that are contrary to nature; and the men likewise gave up natural relations with women and were consumed with passion for one

---

2. Harrison et al, "Conscience," 126.

another, men committing shameless acts with men and receiving in themselves the due penalty for their error. And since they did not see fit to acknowledge God, God gave them up to a debased mind to do what ought not to be done. They were filled with all manner of unrighteousness, evil, covetousness, malice. They are full of envy, murder, strife, deceit, maliciousness. They are gossips, slanderers, haters of God, insolent, haughty, boastful, inventors of evil, disobedient to parents, foolish, faithless, heartless, ruthless. Though they know God's righteous decree that those who practice such things deserve to die, they not only do them but give approval to those who practice them.[3]

Paul wanted to ensure that the fledgling church maintain its conscience, or understand the ramifications of its defilement. The author of Hebrews writes, "Pray for us, for we are sure that we have a clear conscience, desiring to act honorably in all things."[4] Hence, a clear conscience produces honorable behavior.

For these reasons, a Christian leader must adamantly pursue, at all costs, a sanctified conscience before God and man. Again, the conscience is God's gift to all persons, warning them of right and wrong. Unfortunately, perpetual and unrepentant sin can harm the conscience. The Apostle Paul discusses the conscience far more than any other biblical author and informs his young protégé, Timothy, "Now the Spirit expressly says that in later times some will depart from the faith by devoting themselves to deceitful spirits and teachings of demons, through the insincerity of liars whose consciences are seared."[5] This passage clearly states that the conscience can be disregarded and become useless if not properly maintained. Theologian J. I. Packer posits:

> An educated, sensitive conscience is God's monitor. It alerts us to the moral quality of what we do or plan to do, forbids lawlessness and irresponsibility, and makes us feel guilt, shame, and fear of the future retribution, which it tells us we deserve when we have allowed ourselves to defy its restraints. Satan's strategy is to corrupt, desensitize, and if possible kill our consciences. The relativism, materialism, narcissism, secularism, and hedonism of today's Western world help him mightily toward his goal. His task is made

---

3. Rom 1:24–32.
4. Heb 13:18.
5. 1 Tim 4:1–2.

yet simpler by the way in which the world's moral weaknesses have been taken into the contemporary church.[6]

Hence, the conscience must be preserved and nurtured, for the ramifications of harming it bring severe consequences. As the conscience is only as good as the value system with which it is aligned, informing the conscience with morals and ethics based on divine truth will lead the individual to better choices and good behavior.

The word "conscience" derives from the Latin words *scire* and *con*, meaning "to know together," with its Greek counterpart *suneidesis*, meaning "co-knowledge."[7] MacArthur writes, "Conscience is knowledge together with oneself; that is, conscience knows our inner motives and true thoughts. Conscience is above reason and beyond intellect. We may rationalize, trying to justify ourselves in our minds, but a violated conscience will not be easily convinced."[8] The conscience, to some, may seem to be a hindrance based on its killjoy traits. The opposite is true, as it guards the soul against the guilt and consequences of poor decisions by its early warning mechanism. The conscience cannot make a person do what is right, but it may warn of impending danger, giving the individual the opportunity to choose a better path. MacArthur continues:

> The conscience entreats us to do what we believe is right and restrains us from doing what we believe is wrong. The conscience is not equated with the voice of God or the law of God. It is a human faculty that judges our actions and thoughts by the light of the highest standards we perceive. When we violate conscience, it condemns us, triggering feelings of shame, anguish, regret, consternation, anxiety, disgrace, and even fear. When we follow our conscience, it commends us, bringing joy, serenity, self-respect, well-being, and gladness.[9]

Consequently, the Christian leader will do well in being a positive example of Christ when he obeys his conscience, provided his conscience is aligned with biblical truth.

There are thirty occurrences of conscience (*suneidesis*) in the New Testament, which are almost exclusively Pauline. In the following verses, the Apostle Paul presents the importance of keeping a good conscience:

6. Packer, *Rediscovering Holiness*, 151.
7. Henry, *Baker's Dictionary*, 126.
8. MacArthur, *The Vanishing Conscience*, 37.
9. Ibid., 37.

- And looking intently at the council, Paul said, "Brothers, I have lived my life before God in all good conscience up to this day."[10]
- "So I always take pains to have a clear conscience toward both God and man."[11]
- "The aim of our charge is love that issues from a pure heart and a good conscience and a sincere faith."[12]
- "This charge I entrust to you, Timothy, my child, in accordance with the prophecies previously made about you, that by them you may wage the good warfare, holding faith and a good conscience. By rejecting this, some have made shipwreck of their faith."[13]
- "I thank God whom I serve, as did my ancestors, with a clear conscience, as I remember you constantly in my prayers night and day."[14]
- "For our boast is this, the testimony of our conscience, that we behaved in the world with simplicity and godly sincerity, not by earthly wisdom but by the grace of God, and supremely so toward you."[15]

Considering that Paul was formerly a persecutor of Christians and led them to imprisonment and death, the hope of a clean conscience is available to even the worst of sinners who surrender to Christ. The Apostle Peter also provided an imperative on this matter: "Keep a good conscience so that in the thing in which you are slandered, those who revile your good behavior in Christ may be put to shame."[16] The Bible is replete with passages regarding purity, holiness, and a clean conscience. When Paul instructed Timothy on the required attributes for church leaders, he wrote:

> Therefore, an overseer must be above reproach, the husband of one wife, sober-minded, self-controlled, respectable, hospitable, able to teach, not a drunkard, not violent but gentle, not quarrelsome, not a lover of money. He must manage his own household well, with all dignity keeping his children submissive, for if someone does not know how to manage his own household, how will he

10. Acts 23:1.
11. Acts 24:16.
12. 1 Tim 1:5.
13. 1 Tim 1:18-19.
14. 2 Tim 1:3.
15. 2 Cor 1:12.
16. 1 Pet 3:16.

care for God's church? He must not be a recent convert, or he may become puffed up with conceit and fall into the condemnation of the devil. Moreover, he must be well thought of by outsiders, so that he may not fall into disgrace, into a snare of the devil.[17]

It is important to note in this pericope that all the characteristics, outside of "able to teach," are moral qualities produced by one with a clean conscience. Therefore, all Christian leaders, whether serving in secular or Christian vocations, should seek to exemplify these traits of obedience to conscience.

In a postmodern construct, conscience, like all other matters, takes on a very elusive form as each beholder defines it to fit every lifestyle and worldview. In his work *How Can I Develop a Christian Conscience?*, theologian R. C. Sproul writes:

> Historically and classically, the conscience was seen to be our link to the transcendent ethic that resides in God. But with the moral revolution of our culture, a different approach to conscience has emerged, and this is what is called the relativistic view. This is indeed the age of relativism, where values and principles are considered to be mere expressions of the desires and interests of a given group of people at a given time in history. We repeatedly hear that there are no absolutes in our world today. Yet if there are no absolute, transcendent principles, how do we explain this mechanism that we call the conscience? Within a relativistic framework, we see the conscience being defined in evolutionary terms: people's subjective inner personalities are reacting to evolutionary advantageous taboos imposed upon them by their society or by their environment. Having reached a period in our development when these taboos no longer serve to advance our evolution, they can be discarded with nary a thought of the consequences.[18]

It is easy to see the inherent danger in either redefining conscience to allow for all forms of wretched behavior, or worse, deciding that the conscience does not exist. If one can convince (or sear) his conscience into believing that evil is good, then he may act out the worst sorts of evil, without guilt. This is often witnessed in the postmodern era through constant, nefarious terrorist attacks, promotion of the killing of infants inside the mother's womb, the destruction of the traditional family, and the labeling of each sin as a psychological defect. These instances may attempt to be justified by claiming that they were within the bounds of one's conscience, but regrettably,

---

17. 1 Tim 3:1–7.
18. Sproul, *Christian Conscience?*, 10.

the conscience can be so seared that right "becomes" wrong and wrong "becomes" right. This notion was illustrated well in the JFK Jr. airplane crash scenario, in which the correct signals were replaced with faulty ideas.

The collective deadening of societal conscience puts the world on a potential route of no return, outside the intervention of God. As humanity vitiates the elements of guilt and sin, and as Christian leaders become reticent, a culture of degradation and immorality ensues. According to MacArthur:

> Our culture has declared war on guilt. The very concept is considered medieval, obsolete, unproductive. People who trouble themselves with feelings of personal guilt are usually referred to therapists, whose task is to boost their self-image. No one, after all, is supposed to feel guilty. Guilt is not conducive to dignity and self-esteem. Society encourages sin, but it will not tolerate the guilt sin produces.[19]

While this pattern of guiltlessness is prevalent in contemporary culture, Christian leaders must not encompass a dilatory attitude. Instead, they must courageously present truth to a confused people, providing something real and tangible to follow, by pricking the conscience of man with the truth of God.

Although the topic of conscience was commonplace amongst philosophers and theologians for thousands of years, one group took the matter very seriously: the English Puritans. These seventeenth-century stalwarts of the faith were a much-maligned group as they taught and lived out the notion that man exists for one purpose: to serve his Creator. "Puritan," like the designation "Christian," was a pejorative term in its earliest days, and many would still maintain this view. These erudite Christians held a high view of God's sovereignty and elevated his providential will above man's vain attempts at righteousness by works. J. I. Packer writes, "Puritanism was an evangelical holiness movement, seeking to implement its vision of spiritual renewal, national and personal, in the church, in the state, and the home; in education, evangelism, and economics; in individual discipleship and devotion, and in pastoral care and confidence."[20] The Puritans did not equivocate when instructing on matters of sin, heaven, hell, godliness, and man's need to have a right relationship with God through Jesus Christ. They were also very familiar with the idea of conscience and wrote about it often. Puritan Thomas Watson posits, "Self-examination is the setting up

---

19. MacArthur, *The Vanishing Conscience*, 19.
20. Beeke and Pederson, *Meet the Puritans*, xviii.

a court in conscience and keeping a register there, that by strict scrutiny a man may know how things stand between God and his own soul.... A good Christian doth as it were begin the day of Judgment here in his own soul."[21] Watson considered the conscience to be a place where man measures his relationship with God by assessing the clarity of, and obedience to, his conscience.

The Puritans held that guilt and conscience were warning systems for the soul, seeking to protect people from sinful thoughts and behavior. As moral leaders in their day, the Puritans did not strive to be relevant to the world, but instead furthered a countercultural course, adhering to orthodoxy and strongly contending for scriptural inerrancy. While the Puritans lived during the modern era, when empiricism ruled the day, they did not promote an inane belief in God. Rather, they endorsed one with an historical and reasonable foundation. As strong believers in the sufficiency of Scripture, they did not flinch in support of the miracle narratives often mocked by the heathens of their culture. They held that everything written in the Scriptures was factual and the author's (God's) true intention of the text was the only one worthy of consideration. Therefore, as they studied the Bible regarding the conscience, they took the matter to heart; failing to do so would prove destructive to their faith. English Puritan William Fenner draws the following observation relating to the conscience:

> First, we must labour to prevent troubles of conscience by taking heed that we do nothing contrary to conscience ... Nothing that we get in any evil way will cheer and comfort us in time of need.... Secondly, if we will maintain our peace we must labor to have our hearts grounded in the assurance of the love of God ... Thirdly, we must use the exercise of faith in applying the blood of Christ. We must labour[sic] to purge and cleanse our consciences with it. If we find that we have sinned we must run presently [that is, immediately] to the blood of Christ to wash away our sin. We must not let the wound fester or exulcerate [become an infected sore] but presently [that is, immediately] get it healed ... As we sin daily, so he justifieth daily, and we must daily go to him for it ... We must every day eye the brazen serpent. Justification is an ever-running fountain, and therefore we cannot look to have all the water at once ... O let us then sue out a daily pardon ... Let us not sleep one night without a new pardon. Better sleep in a house full of adders and venomous beasts than sleep in

---

21. Watson, *Heaven Taken by Storm*, 40.

one sin. O then be sure with the day to clear the sins of the day. Then shall our conscience have true peace.[22]

Fenner's graphic illustration of the adders and beasts suggests an urgency and fearfulness that one should have about continually cleansing and sanctifying the conscience. This realistic declaration of man's sinfulness brings encouragement to the leader struggling with sin, as hope and redemption are found through the blood of Christ. The quiet conscience is one which is right before God and prepared to serve man. According to Puritan Reformed Theological Seminary President Joel Beeke:

> The restoration of the conscience is part of the process of sanctification that begins with regeneration and does not end until we enter glory. It is a work of God's grace that we must seek in prayer. The most significant means is to place ourselves under the sound and searching preaching of both the law and the gospel. As Sibbes said, the steps to a good conscience are first to be troubled by our sins, second to find peace by trusting in Christ, and third to resolve to please God in all things. With these three elements active in our lives, we are positioned to grow more in a good conscience as we live by faith for God's pleasure. The most critical attitude is honesty and humility before God, for conscience always confronts us with the truth that God is Lord.[23]

A pure conscience, then, is one which is cleansed by God after repentance. A right conscience is equipped to produce correct behavior. For the Christian leader, this provides courage under fire and confidence to take a stand on truth. In the words of nineteenth-century Scottish theologian James Buchanon,

> In convincing of sin, the Spirit of God, acting agreeably to the moral constitution of our nature, takes the conscience as the subject of his operations, and seeks to enlighten, quicken, and invigorate it by the light and power of divine truth. It is the conscience that is the subject of his operations. It is the moral faculty, the faculty of discriminating betwixt right and wrong, which makes us fit subjects for the convincing work of the Spirit. Had we no conscience, we should be incapable of moral convictions, as are the living but irresponsible beasts of the field and fowls of the air.[24]

---

22. Fenner, *Souls Looking-Glasse*, 134.
23. Challies, "The Christian Conscience," 919–25.
24. Buchanan, *Holy Spirit*, 116.

The Leadership Imperative

These scriptural examples alluded to by Vincent present a divine capability of strength for the leader which would otherwise not be available. A pusillanimous leader, therefore, will be ineffective and likely to cause more harm than good to his followers.

Because sin is so pervasive, a clean conscience may be ephemeral, requiring continued prayer and contrition. The Puritans wrote and often preached about the nature of the conscience. The following excerpts from their works present the visceral nature of their beliefs:

- "A good conscience is the best divinity"—Thomas Fuller[25]
- "If we take care to keep a good conscience, we may leave it to God to take care of our good name"—Matthew Henry[26]
- "A good conscience and a good name is like a gold ring set with a rich diamond."—Thomas Watson[27]
- "It is our *overseer* as it governs our entire life, and it is our *mirror* as it makes known to us in what terms we stand with God"—Robert Harris[28]

Each of these quotes adds to the prism of conscience in its multifaceted understanding and application. The Puritans revealed God as the originator of the conscience which reminds, warns, and validates one's thoughts, temptations, and actions.

The amelioration of a strong conscience was also noted often by the Puritan predecessors, the Protestant Reformers. Although the Reformers were significant in number, two of the most exceptional leaders of this movement are Martin Luther and John Calvin. Each of these men paved the way for their future Puritan brethren on matters of grace, holiness, faith, soteriology, and conscience. In his classic work *Institutes of the Christian Religion*, John Calvin presents his case for the genesis and purpose of the conscience:

> For just as when through the mind and understanding men grasp a knowledge of things, and from this are said "to know," this is the source of the word "knowledge," so also when they have a sense of divine judgment, as a witness joined to them, which does not

---

25. Fuller, *Gnomologia*, 6.
26. Henry, *Commentary*.
27. Watson, *Discourse*, 350.
28. Harris, *The Works*.

allow them to hide their sins from being accused before the Judge's tribunal, this sense is called "conscience." For it is a certain mean between God and man because it does not allow man to suppress within himself what he knows, but pursues him to the point of convicting him . . . Therefore this awareness which hales man before God's judgment is a sort of guardian appointed for man to note and spy out all his secrets that nothing may be buried in darkness.[29]

The protection aspect of the conscience to which Calvin refers is noteworthy as it may keep one from making poor or sinful decisions with considerable consequences.

Martin Luther, who is viewed as the father of the Protestant Reformation, contended as a priest against the Roman Catholic Church of which he served. After struggling with his own sin and guilt, and never finding peace in his repetitive priestly confessions and works of contrition, he eagerly studied the Bible to better understand the mind of God. During his studies in the book of Hebrews, he came across a verse which changed the course of his life, "The just shall live by faith."[30] This verse revealed to him that works could not merit salvation as it was only by faith in Jesus Christ and by his grace that humanity is saved. As Luther continued his studies, his conscience became very sensitive to divine truth, and he spent the remainder of his life defending it. After being summoned to the Diet of Worms to answer to the accusations of blasphemy against the Roman Church, he was commanded to recant his written works against the Catholic Church and his accusations against the church, as contained in his ninety-five theses. After much struggle, Luther responded with these famous words:

> Because your serene majesty and your lordships seek a simple answer, I will give it in this manner, neither horned nor toothed. Unless I am convinced by the testimony of the Scriptures or by clear reason (for I do not trust either in the pope or in councils alone, because we well know that they have often erred and contradicted themselves), I am bound by the Scriptures I have quoted. My conscience is captive to the Word of God. I cannot and I will not retract anything, because it is neither safe nor right to go against conscience.[31]

Luther's leadership and courage in the face of excommunication and death changed the course of church history. It opened wide the doors of the

---

29. Calvin, *Institutes*, III.19.15.
30. Heb 10:38 (KJV).
31. Spitz, *Protestant Reformation*, 75.

written word, the Bible, which would eventually be translated into many languages, and thereby impact the world for Christ.

If Luther had not informed and adhered to his conscience, it is hard to know what the church of Christ would look like today. Luther later elaborated on his view of the conscience:

> Conscience is not the power to do works, but to judge them. The proper work of conscience (as Paul says in Romans 2:15), is to accuse or excuse, to make guilty or guiltless, uncertain or certain. Its purpose is not to do, but to pass judgment on what has been done and what should be done, and this judgment makes us stand accused or saved in God's sight.[32]

Christian leaders can look to Martin Luther and many other faithful saints through the ages as examples to follow about acquiring, maintaining, and acting upon a clean conscience. Although the path of a pure conscience may be the most difficult option and provide the least amount of temporal satisfaction, the long-term benefits to the soul and to outside observers may be powerful. The Puritans and Reformers have much to teach those living in postmodernity. These men of old held firm to the meanings of words and diligently lived by them. They did not question the multitude of biblical passages regarding the conscience, but instead, they committed themselves to informing their consciences based on Divine Truth. While this idea is largely unpopular in the postmodern era, it is still just as efficacious today as it has been throughout history. Consequently, Christian leaders who inform the conscience and lead accordingly will do much good in elevating truth in a time when people are busy trying to define it.

---

32. Zachman, *The Assurance of Faith*, 28.

4

Vocational Leadership

A Sacred Calling

> *For even when we were with you, we would give you this command: If anyone is not willing to work, let him not eat. For we hear that some among you walk in idleness, not busy at work, but busybodies. Now such persons we command and encourage in the Lord Jesus Christ to do their work quietly and to earn their own living.*
>
> —2 THESSALONIANS 3:10-12

THE TERMS "VOCATION" OR "work" in the postmodern era are all too often considered in the pejorative, as they suggest getting up early, working late, submitting to authority, dealing with obstreperous peers, and continual uncertainty. This negative view was never the design for work; in fact, work was created as a blessing from God to Adam and Eve at creation. Some hold that work was a result of Adam's sin, but the biblical account provides a different narrative. The Genesis pericope records, "The Lord God took the man and put him in the garden of Eden to work it and keep it. And the Lord God commanded the man, saying, 'You may surely eat of every tree of the garden, but of the tree of the knowledge of good and evil you shall not eat, for in the day that you eat of it you shall surely die.'"[1] It is important to keep

---

1. Gen 2:15–17.

the chronology of this account in perspective to see that Adam was placed in the garden to "work it and keep it" *before* he was given the imperative to refrain from eating the fruit. Hence, God designed work to be part of the sin-free world and, as such, something to be enjoyed. In her work *Creed or Chaos*, Dorothy Sayers writes:

> Christian work is not a specific type of occupation but rather an attitude which sees work "not primarily as a thing one does to live, but the thing one lives to do." Work is, or it should be, the full expression of the worker's gifts, the thing in which he finds spiritual, mental and bodily satisfaction, and the medium in which he offers himself to God.[2]

Although Adam and Eve were the only humans to experience this satisfaction to its fullest in a sin-free world, the blessing of work is still available today for those who desire to embrace it.

Unfortunately, Adam disobeyed the command from God not to eat the forbidden fruit, making work a hardship, as exemplified in a strong rebuke from God:

> And to Adam he said, Because you have listened to the voice of your wife and have eaten of the tree of which I commanded you, "You shall not eat of it, cursed is the ground because of you; in pain you shall eat of it all the days of your life; thorns and thistles it shall bring forth for you; and you shall eat the plants of the field. By the sweat of your face, you shall eat bread, till you return to the ground, for out of it you were taken; for you are dust, and to dust you shall return."[3]

This tragic turning point in history tainted everything on earth moving forward, including the extent of blessing in work. Roels writes,

> Sadly, the fall into sin severely damaged our ability to connect imaginative and energetic work with the cultivation of creation. The perfect balance of joyous work and creation abundance is destroyed through original human disobedience. The filling of the garden is replaced with the tilling of a coarse, weed-filled world and with the curse that "by the sweat of your face you shall eat bread" (Gen 3:19). Efforts to cultivate and create become stained by corrupted talents and impure motivations; the desires that

---

2. Sayers, *Creed or Chaos?*, 53.
3. Gen 3:17–19.

match these damaged gifts are distorted; the process of exchange is fraught with ethical challenges.[4]

Veith also provides a dire view of this transformative time, "Our vocations, like the rest of the earth, are under a curse, one directed explicitly at marriage, childbirth, and work (Gen 3:16–19). Adam and Eve were driven out of Paradise, and a cherubim keeps us out with a flaming sword (3:22–24); so we can expect no utopia."[5] Although sin transformed work from being pure joy to being a task requiring extensive labor and hardship, it is no less a gift from God to humanity for productively occupying time on earth. With honest labor comes a sense of fulfillment and honor. This joy can be witnessed on long-term projects, such as ship building, where thousands of workers use their skills to produce something which will one day sail the oceans with hundreds aboard.

Work aids in assigning purpose to one's life in the form of a mission, a calling, something to eagerly pursue. Dostoevsky, in *The Brothers Karamazov* pens, "For the secret of man's being is not only to live . . . but to live for something definite. Without a firm notion of what he is living for, man will not accept life and will rather destroy himself than remain on earth."[6] Dostoevsky poignantly expresses the meaninglessness of life when one has nothing to pursue. Vocation provides such meaning, as one may find fulfillment and joy at working and producing something of value. Christian leaders are to pursue godliness in all their activities, including vocation, and this is accomplished by emulating the character and actions of Christ. As an equal part of the Trinity, work was modeled by Jesus Christ throughout the six-day creation account (John 1:1–5), setting an example for everyone to follow. To imitate Christ, then, is to work in a way which honors God. As said by Grudem:

> One way that we can glorify God is often overlooked. This additional way to glorify God is the key to understanding why God made the world the way He did. It is also a key to understanding why human beings have an instinctive drive to work, to be productive, to invent, to earn and save and give, and to do the thousands of specific activities that fill our days. This additional way to glorify God is imitation—imitation of the attributes of God.[7]

---

4. Roels, "The Christian Calling", 357–69.
5. Veith, *God at Work*, 143.
6. Fyodor Dostoyevsky, *The Karamazov Brothers*, 13.
7. Grudem, *Business*, 13.

To lead others most effectively, the leader himself requires an example to follow. For the Christian leader, Jesus Christ is the perfect example; the apostles and prophets are also godly men whom one should imitate. A strong work ethic is a consistent trait among the greatest Christian leaders throughout time.

The postmodern era has sought to deconstruct the concept of vocation as something to be sought after, enjoyed, and embraced. In fact, postmodernity has resulted in shifting many work schedules from a forty-hour work week to thirty hours or less, often with the government providing for those who choose not to work. Marxism, socialism, and some unions have all sought to trample competitiveness, overpay employees, and vilify management. The destruction of these ideas can be witnessed throughout modern and postmodern eras in the collapse of every nation which has embraced these ideals. As the opening Scripture passage of this chapter indicates, those who choose not to work should also not eat. Unfortunately, many governments have usurped God's command for people to work and have removed the masses' incentive by creating a culture of entitlement for those who choose "idleness." In 2015, the United States Census Bureau reported that a remarkable fifty-two million citizens, or 21.3 percent of the population, relied on government assistance programs.[8] This number is continually rising, as depending upon the government to meet basic human needs is an accepted norm in postmodern times. Unfortunately, this negation of work as a means of purpose and sustainment results in increased crime, alcoholism, gang activity, and hopelessness. The book of Proverbs presents a clear distinction between the wise and the foolish work ethic:

- Like vinegar to the teeth and smoke to the eyes, so is the sluggard to those who send him;[9]
- Whoever is slack in his work is a brother to him who destroys;[10]
- Slothfulness casts into a deep sleep, and an idle person will suffer hunger;[11]

---

8. "21.3 Percent," lines 1–2.
9. Prov 10:26.
10. Prov 18:9.
11. Prov 19:15.

- Love not sleep, lest you come to poverty; open your eyes, and you will have plenty of bread;[12]
- The desire of the sluggard kills him, for his hands refuse to labor. All day long he craves and craves, but the righteous gives and does not hold back.[13]

Vocation bears a much deeper meaning than the postmodern era appreciates and brings with it a great call to action. Roels provides an excellent synopsis to consider:

> The word vocation itself is rooted in the Latin *vocare*: to call. Vocation implies a relationship to the one who calls us. Biblically, this caller is the triune God, the author of creation, redemption, and renewal. This trinitarian caller asks each person to respond to the voice of God, as Scripture illuminates it through the story of creation, the experience of Israel, the work of Jesus, and the history of the church.[14]

Roels's biblical and logical conclusion reveals vocation to be much grander than the day-to-day tasks involved, regardless of the type of work performed, as its source is God himself. When one comprehends that God is calling him to vocation, the job description itself is quickly relegated to second place. When the Apostle Paul writes, "Only let each person lead the life that the Lord has assigned to him, and to which God has called him,"[15] he has in mind the calling to work, or vocation, which God assigns to each of his children as a means of grace. This Exodus pericope gives the reader insight into the detailed nature to which God calls people to work:

> Then Moses said to the people of Israel, "See, the Lord has called by name Bezalel the son of Uri, son of Hur, of the tribe of Judah; and he has filled him with the Spirit of God, with skill, with intelligence, with knowledge, and with all craftsmanship, to devise artistic designs, to work in gold and silver and bronze, in cutting stones for setting, and in carving wood, for work in every skilled craft. And he has inspired him to teach, both him and Oholiab the son of Ahisamach of the tribe of Dan. He has filled them with skill to do every sort of work done by an engraver or by a designer or by an

---

12. Prov 20:13.
13. Prov 21:25–26.
14. Roels, "The Christian Calling," 357–69.
15. 1 Cor 7:17.

embroiderer in blue and purple and scarlet yarns and fine twined linen, or by a weaver—by any sort of workman or skilled designer."[16]

While it may be tempting to consider talents as originating with man's own efforts and hard work, this passage illustrates the very profound nature of God's very specific calling; equipping men and women to service is part of his elective will. The Apostle Paul writes, "Now there are varieties of gifts, but the same Spirit; and there are varieties of service, but the same Lord; and there are varieties of activities, but it is the same God who empowers them all in everyone."[17] Paul desired that his hearers would never gloat in their talents as if they had created them, but that they would understand of the purpose of the gifts, which is to serve God.

While the overall trajectory toward a strong work ethic appears unfavorable, some positive movements have also occurred. Though some of the points on the following chart displaying the transition from the modern to the postmodern era may be disputed, most appear to be universally accepted and provide some positive movement.

Table I: Modern Versus Postmodern Principles of Management[18]

	MODERN	POSTMODERN
Planning	1. Short-term profit goals	1. Long-term profit goals
	2. Mass production	2. Flexible production
	3. Worker is a cost	3. Worker is an investment
	4. Vertical planning	4. Horizontal planning
	5. Top-down focus	5. Internal and external customer focus
	6. Planning leads to order	6. Planning leads to disorder and confusion

---

16. Exod 35:30–35.
17. 1 Cor 12:4–6.
18. Boje and Dennehy, *Managing*, xxix.

Vocational Leadership

Organizing

1. One man, one job, and de-skilled jobs
2. Labor-management confrontation
3. Division of departments
4. Tall is better
5. Homogeneity is strength
6. Top has voice and diversity is tolerated
7. Efficiency increases with specialization, formalization, routinization, fragmentation, division of labor

1. Work teams, multi-skilled workers
2. Labor-management cooperation
3. Flexible networks with permeable boundaries
4. Flat is better
5. Diversity is strength
6. Many voices and diversity is an asset
7. Efficiency decreases with specialization, formalization, routinization, fragmentation, and division of labor

Influencing

1. Authority vested in superior
2. Extrinsic rewards and punishments
3. Surveillance mechanisms everywhere
4. Women paid 68 percent of men; minorities paid less
5. Discourse is white-male-based
6. Individual incentives

1. Authority delegated to leaders by teams
2. Intrinsic, empowered ownership over work process
3. People are self-disciplined
4. Women and minorities equally paid
5. Polyvocal/polylogic discourse
6. Team incentives

Leading

1. Theory X or Y
2. Centralized with many layers and rules
3. Boss-centered
4. White male career tracks
5. Tell them what to do

1. Theory S (Servant Leadership)
2. Decentralized with few layers and wide spans
3. People-centered
4. Tracks for women and minorities
5. Visionary

	1. Centralized control	1. Decentralized control
	2. End-of-line inspection	2. Quality control is everyone's job
	3. Micro surveillance	3. Two-way surveillance
	4. Red tape	4. Cut red tape
Controlling	5. Lots of procedures, rules, MBO, and computers for surveillance	5. Dump procedures
	6. Train top of pyramid	6. Train people
	7. Measure result criteria	7. Measure process criteria
	8. Hoard information	8. Information is given to all
	9. Fear-based controls	9. Self-control

This graphic portrays both positive and negative trending from a biblical perspective. For Christian leaders, these new norms provide insight into the thinking of postmodernists, helping them to lead properly. Even the movement from vertical to horizontal control should be embraced by offering more opportunity for employees to flourish without heavy oversight. These new patterns should provide a ray of optimism to leaders who find themselves discouraged at the work ethic of so many in today's workforce. As Grudem alluded, "Human beings have an instinctive drive to work, to be productive, to invent, to earn and save and give."[19] These inherent desires for productivity need to be explored and encouraged instead of stifled through appeasement approaches which elevate laziness out of a fear of offending. The Christian leader who expresses his enthusiasm and gratefulness for work is being a wise example, worthy to be emulated.

While some in the faith have historically viewed Christian vocation as merely pertaining to church leadership,[20] the Scriptures make it clear that any honorable labor meets the definition. The Protestant Reformation was a historical turning point in bringing people back to a biblical idea of work. Per Nel and Scholtz:

19. Grudem, *Business*, 13.
20. Placher, "Callings," 2.

> Luther's discovery that we are saved by God's grace and not by our own works initiated a series of momentous events during the Protestant Reformation. Relevant to the current discussion, it cut through the two-tiered spirituality of the medieval world, which distinguished between the laity and the clergy, the ordinary Christian and the monk. Luther proclaimed the priesthood of all believers. Not only some but all Christians have a vocation, not only in the sense of a call to faith but also as a call to serve God and one's neighbour[sic] in a concrete way.[21]

It is noteworthy that some lines of work are immoral as they rebel against the law of God. However, these areas are few, and the worthy fields of vocation include any secular or Christian endeavor to which one is committed. The Free Presbyterian Church Journal notes:

> Before the Reformation, it was believed that the only way to serve God was by taking holy orders and removing yourself from the normal world. People with "ordinary" jobs were viewed as second class citizens, and this led to a two-tier system of clergy and laity. The Reformation changed this. It was accepted that all work and activity that was not sinful could and should be done to the glory of God—whether a plough boy or dish-washer, a shelf stacker or barista, a managing director, or consultant surgeon. God calls people to different roles, situations, and seasons in life, so that He can be glorified in all places, at all times. Since it is God's eternal purpose that His people live to praise His glory (Ephesians 1:6), it is therefore the Christian's responsibility in life to do all to the glory of God. Remember, *"Whether therefore ye eat, or drink, or whatsoever ye do, do all to the glory of God."* (1 Cor 10:31)[22]

These vocations, then, are far more than physical and mental labors; they are ministries by which God is glorified. Witherington notes, "Work, whether it involves plumbing a sink or plumbing the depths of the cosmos, in the hands of a Christian is ministry of all believers . . . Work is an extension of Christ's ministry and the ministry he called his original disciples to do. This, of course, can involve a plethora of activities and professions."[23] Work, therefore, is a God-given privilege used to bring him glory regardless of the actual tasking. The Apostle Paul makes this point clear as he encourages the believers in Colossae, "Whatever you do, work heartily, as for the Lord and

---

21. Nel and Scholtz, "Calling."
22. Free Presbyterian, "Why?", 28.
23. Witherington, *Work*, 14.

not for men, knowing that from the Lord you will receive the inheritance as your reward. You are serving the Lord Christ."[24] Christian vocation is never bifurcated into secular and religious work, as all honorable labor in the hands of a follower of Christ must be considered sacred.

Accordingly, Christian leaders are wise to ensure the utmost integrity in their labors, setting an example for others to follow. Witherington adds, "Work is not a secular activity; it is a sacred one originally ordained by God, and so it must be undertaken in holy ways. And there is absolutely nothing wrong with good, old-fashioned honest labor or hard work, including manual labor. But whatever we do, we are to strive for excellence."[25] The lesson in this for leaders is to never elevate one type of work over another in an organization, although the responsibilities and pay structures may differ. Each employee should be treated with great respect, as all work accomplished with honesty, vigor, and verve should be honored. These actions will produce employees who know that their labors are appreciated and respected, resulting in higher morale, retention, and productivity. Paul, in his letter to the Romans, provides this warning:

> For by the grace given to me I say to everyone among you not to think of himself more highly than he ought to think, but to think with sober judgment, each according to the measure of faith that God has assigned. For as in one body we have many members, and the members do not all have the same function, so we, though many, are one body in Christ, and individually members one of another. Having gifts that differ according to the grace given to us, let us use them: if prophecy, in proportion to our faith; if service, in our serving; the one who teaches, in his teaching; the one who exhorts, in his exhortation; the one who contributes, in generosity; the one who leads, with zeal; the one who does acts of mercy, with cheerfulness.[26]

Paul presents the argument that, while various types of work are acquired, all are needed equally and should be honored accordingly. This removes any temptation for one to look down upon another due to the perceived irrelevance of his work. One of the dirtiest vocations is trash collection, but one would not want to live in a society without this profession, as it serves a very important function for humanity.

---

24. Col 3:23:24.
25. Witherington, *Work*, 15.
26. Rom 12:3–11.

Vocational Leadership

Furthermore, God-honoring, honest work sets an example to the prevailing postmodern culture to consider. Gene Veith, the author of *God at Work: Your Christian Vocation in All of Life*, writes:

> The doctrine of vocation amounts to a comprehensive doctrine of the Christian life, having to do with faith and sanctification, grace and good works. It is a key to Christian ethics. It shows how Christians can influence culture. It transfigures ordinary, everyday life with the presence of God . . . The priesthood of all believers did not make everyone into church workers; rather it turned every kind of work into a sacred calling.[27]

The natural result of Christian vocation is filling the great commission in the workplace. Using the light metaphor, Jesus Christ encourages the faithful to honorable work in a dark world, "You are the light of the world. A city set on a hill cannot be hidden. Nor do people light a lamp and put it under a basket, but on a stand, and it gives light to all in the house. In the same way, let your light shine before others, so that they may see your good works and give glory to your Father who is in heaven."[28]

Christian leaders in their vocations do well to keep their focus much higher than the daily profit sheets, stock numbers, and product sales. Instead, placing Christ first in all activities will produce eternal results. Witherington posits:

> Regarding vocation, every Christian has a primary obligation to fulfill the Great Commandment and Great Commission. This is "job one." There are secondary callings we may be called to in addition to this—being doctors, lawyers, business people, ministers, parents, etc. But they are indeed secondary callings. Our primary task as persons recreated in the image of Christ is to do the very thing Christ came to earth to do—share the Good News of salvation, healing, the coming Kingdom. There are a variety of ways, venues, and avenues for accomplishing the primary task, and it can be accomplished in tandem with and even by means of the secondary callings or tasks.[29]

The secondary calling is an important one, but should always yield to the primary, even as the potential temptation for wealth and power grows.

---

27. Veith, *God at Work*, 17.
28. Matt 5:14–16.
29. Witherington, *Work*, 46.

The Leadership Imperative

As described in this chapter, vocation is a calling from God and as such becomes a sacred endeavor. It is also important to note that vocation is not the only calling and must be one part of the Christian's walk, not its entirety. Even Christian leaders who embrace vocation as a sacred calling must be cautious that it does not become an idol. Other callings for the Christian involve family, church, and evangelizing the lost. Each of these must maintain a proper balance so that each may honor Christ accordingly. Veith notes:

> Today, even Protestant Christians have often slipped into the assumption that serving God is a matter of church work or spiritual exercises. Churches set up programs that can take up every night of the week. Some Christians are so busy doing church activities, making evangelism calls, or going to Bible studies that they neglect their spouses and children. Some Christians are preoccupied with the Lord's work while letting their marriages fall apart, ignoring the needs of their children, and otherwise sinning against the actual responsibilities to which God has called them. According to the doctrine of vocation, the Church is the place where Christians meet every week to find the forgiveness of Christ, feed on God's Word, and grow in their faith. Then they are sent out into their vocations—to their spouses, children, jobs, and culture—for that faith to bear fruit.[30]

Veith's balanced perspective on the Christian's calling should serve as a warning to those who place an overabundance of time and energy on one aspect of service while overlooking the rest. By nature, vocation is not a fortuitous effort. but must be carefully planned, managed, and prayed over. This is especially true for those who serve in positions of leadership that they might be a powerful example of faithfulness to peers, employees, spouses, children, neighbors, and the unbelieving world. Work, family, and vocational balance is an important task, as the pendulum can move from one extreme to the next while often causing lasting damage to those left behind. Christian leaders have a greater obligation to seek equilibrium, as each facet of calling requires full attention. A workaholic will likely have a spouse and children lacking affection, while one who spends too much time in lay ministry may lose sight of his other vocational callings.

Although much of this chapter is devoted to a strong work ethic, it is important also to note that too much work can prove to be just as disastrous as laziness. Witherington posits, "One of the most pervasive pathologies in

---

30. Veith, "Vocation," 119.

our culture today is the tendency to work to excess, without proper rest."[31] Even if a sense of balance is achieved in the various sacred callings, rest must also be part of the schedule. The six-day creation account culminated with a day of rest, as God was setting an example for his people to follow. The human body is designed both to work and to rest, and each of them must be taken seriously for the work to be efficacious. Consequently, prioritization of callings must be continually assessed and the leader must also acquire flexibility, allowing God to move him in another direction if necessary. The negative results of overworking include stress, sickness, disease, lack of family time, hindered worship, and lack of availability to serve in other ways. While work is a good thing and must be revered, so also are the other callings of God on one's life. Worship, family time, recreation, serving others, and work should be planned in such a way that complement, rather than oppose, one another. Each of these facets of life are given to man to glorify God with the skills, abilities, and grace which he bestowed upon his creation.

---

31. Witherington, *Work*, 46.

5

Leading by Loving
The Agape Supremacy

There is no light in the planet but that which cometh from the sun; there is no light in the moon but that which is borrowed, and there is no true love in the heart but that which cometh from God. Love is the light, the life, and way of the universe. Now, God is both life, and light, and way, and, to crown all, God is love. From this overflowing fountain of the infinite love of God, all our love to God must spring. This must ever be a great and certain truth, that we love him, for no other reason than because he first loved us.

—C. H. SPURGEON[1]

IN HIS ACCLAIMED WORK, *The Four Loves*, C. S. Lewis writes:

> There is no safe investment. To love at all is to be vulnerable. Love anything, and your heart will certainly be wrung and possibly be broken. If you want to make sure of keeping it intact, you must give your heart to no one, not even to an animal. Wrap it carefully round with hobbies and little luxuries; avoid all entanglements; lock it up safe in the casket or coffin of your selfishness. But in that casket—safe, dark, motionless, airless—it will change. It will not be broken; it will become unbreakable, impenetrable, irredeemable. The alternative to tragedy, or at least to the risk of tragedy, is damnation. The

---

1. Spurgeon, "Love," para. 5.

only place outside Heaven where you can be perfectly safe from all the dangers and perturbations of love is Hell.[2]

Although the volumes written on the topic of leadership are pervasive, it is rare to find one which focuses on *love* as an integral attribute. Even the writings on Christian leadership focus very little, if at all, on the need for leaders to love their followers. This is unfortunate, as the foundation of Christianity is based on a God of love, namely, Jesus Christ. Understanding the perfect love which is exemplified by Christ provides insight and wisdom to the Christian leader, whether his environment is secular or sacred. As most Christian leaders work in secular settings, the application of Christ's ministry is fitting, for he spent much time teaching and leading people of various backgrounds and beliefs. Christ's ministry focus was on the sick (sinner) and not the healthy (Mark 2:17). Hence, the evangelistic leadership focus should also be on reaching the sick, while at the same time encouraging the healthy. The christological emphasis on love was evident throughout Jesus' life; he sacrificed his own life so that wretched sinners could become glorified saints. Similarly, Christian leaders must have a deep love which seeks the best in others, even to the point of sacrifice.

Ted Engstrom, the author of the classic work *The Making of a Christian Leader*, elaborates on the example of Christ:

> His kind of service set an example. He was willing to wash His disciple's feet. His perfect, sinless, human life ended in self-sacrifice at Calvary. Thus he showed His followers how to serve, and he demanded no less of those who would carry on His work on earth. Jesus teaches all leaders for all time that greatness is not found in rank or position but in service. He makes it clear that true leadership is grounded in love which must issue in service.[3]

Engstrom shows that love is a call to action, a call to serve, and a call to sacrifice. Leaders are often confronted with those who appear to be "unlovable" due to their actions, words, intentions, and attitudes. The example of Christ also deals with this matter as the Apostle Paul explains: "but God shows his love for us in that while we were still sinners, Christ died for us."[4] Christ died for his future followers, not because of anything inherently

---

2. Lewis, *The Four Loves*, 121.
3. Engstrom, *Making*, 37.
4. Rom 5:8.

good in them, but because he loved them (2 Tim 1:9). Michael calls this "redemptive leadership":

> A redemptive leader is characterized by "unconditional love." Unconditional love says, "You have done nothing and can do nothing that will prevent my loving you." This does not mean that you condone one's actions or wink at sin. If a moral failure occurs, you must address it. If a relationship fails, you must confront it. If someone fails in a responsibility, you must correct that person.[5]

The redemptive love perfected by Christ is the example for all Christian leaders to follow.

Love in the postmodern era has been consigned to nothing more than a feeling or a strong emotion. For this reason, divorce in the United States, once taboo, is now promoted, accepted, and even celebrated. Men and women often enter the covenant of marriage with the notion that love is a feeling, but it does not take long for the "feelings" to ebb and flow amidst the challenges of life. If a relationship is based on this assessment of love, the likelihood of marital success is bleak. However, if one discovers the true meaning of love, with its foundation in serving one another, successful marriage, life, and the ability to bless others is well within reach. The Pauline literature spends much time in explaining love in detail, dispelling the postmodern notion of love being a mere feeling or emotion. As the Apostle Paul seeks to encourage and admonish a group of Corinthian believers who have embraced a worldly and fleshly view of love, he writes:

> If I speak in the tongues of men and of angels, but have not love, I am a noisy gong or a clanging cymbal. And if I have prophetic powers, and understand all mysteries and all knowledge, and if I have all faith, so as to remove mountains, but have not love, I am nothing. If I give away all I have, and if I deliver up my body to be burned, but have not love, I gain nothing. Love is patient and kind; love does not envy or boast; it is not arrogant or rude. It does not insist on its own way; it is not irritable or resentful; it does not rejoice at wrongdoing, but rejoices with the truth. Love bears all things, believes all things, hopes all things, endures all things.[6]

The Corinthian culture was much like the postmodern era, for hedonism and self-interests were paramount. According to MacArthur,

---

5. Michael, *Spurgeon on Leadership*, 138.
6. 1 Cor 13:1–7.

Leading by Loving

The Corinthian Christians were not walking in the Spirit. They were selfish, self-designing, self-willed, self-motivated, and doing everything possible to promote their own interests and welfare. Everyone was doing his own things for his own good, with little or no regard for others . . . Among the many things those believers lacked, the most significant was love.[7]

Few would doubt that this same culture is pervasive today, which makes this pericope very timely in its application. If a Christian leader wishes to internally assess his love for others, replacing the word *love* from 1 Corinthians 13:4–7 with one's own name may provide valuable insight.

Writing for the *Inside Business Journal*, David Boisselle from Regent University provides a useful point-by-point assessment of this passage as it relates to leadership:

1. Love is patient. A person who leads with love does not lose patience with his or her people. It's never, "I'll give you one more chance."
2. Love is kind. Kindness does not mean "giving in" to an associate's wishes; sometimes kindness may be extended by an act of "tough love."
3. Love is not jealous. Leading with love means desiring and celebrating the success of others.
4. Love does not brag. Leading with love means letting your work speak for itself.
5. Love is not arrogant. Leading with love means servant leadership, not grasping for power.
6. Love does not act unbecomingly. Leading with love means building others up.
7. Love does not seek its own. Leading with love means it's not about you.
8. Love is not provoked. Leading with love means maintaining an even temperament. Everyone has a bad day now and then, don't we?
9. Love does not take into account a wrong suffered. Leading with love means not keeping score. Let it go and live to work together another day.
10. Love does not rejoice in unrighteousness. Leading with love means dwelling on the positives of people, not their negatives.

7. MacArthur, *1 Corinthians*, 327.

11. Love rejoices with the truth. Leading with love means trafficking in the truth and integrity at all times.

12. Love bears all things. Leading with love means supporting others not only when they are prospering, but especially when they need you to pick them up.

13. Love believes all things. Leading with love means extending the benefit of the doubt.

14. Love hopes all things. Leading with love means never losing faith in our people, hoping for and expecting the best from them.

15. Love endures all things. Anyone can lead through good times; we lead with love when the going becomes toughest.[8]

Boisselle reveals that every aspect of *agape* love as described by the Apostle Paul is applicable and essential to Christian leadership. These fifteen principles provide a plethora of areas by which a leader may evaluate his leadership acumen based on biblical principles. The passage in 1 Corinthians further debunks the notion that love is merely a feeling and shows it is an act of one's resolve, requiring purposeful intent. While wonderful feelings may and often do accompany loving behavior, they are byproducts of obedience and not love itself.

Love, therefore, always yields to the betterment of others, even to the point of sacrificing self-interests. MacArthur continues: "Love is above all sacrificial. It is sacrifice of self for the sake of others, even for others who may care nothing at all for us and who may even hate us. It is not a feeling but a determined act of will, which always results in determined acts of self-giving. Love is the willing, joyful desire to put the welfare of others above our own."[9] This explanation of love is comforting to leaders who are confronted with obstreperous employees or other followers who continually seek to belittle or demean them and their authority. Action always follows biblical love. As MacArthur notes, it is "a determined act of will, which always results in determined acts of self-giving."[10] All christological and apostolic writings support the basis of genuine love in the verb tense, meaning it is an "action" instead of a nebulous notion.

---

8. Boisselle, "Love, the Killer App, Works."
9. MacArthur, *1 Corinthians*, 329.
10. Ibid.

Leading by Loving

The Scriptures provide three terms to describe various forms of love including *eros, philia,* and *agape. Eros* signifies a sexual desire, *phili* designates a brotherly love, and *agape* is the supreme form of love as illustrated in Christ's sacrificial death.[11] It is *agape* love that Christ questioned Peter about in the famous Johannine "Do you love me?" discourse:

> When they had finished breakfast, Jesus said to Simon Peter, "Simon, son of John, do you love me more than these?" He said to him, "Yes, Lord; you know that I love you." He said to him, "Feed my lambs." He said to him a second time, "Simon, son of John, do you love me?" He said to him, "Yes, Lord; you know that I love you." He said to him, "Tend my sheep." He said to him the third time, "Simon, son of John, do you love me?" Peter was grieved because he said to him the third time, "Do you love me?" and he said to him, "Lord, you know everything; you know that I love you." Jesus said to him, "Feed my sheep."[12]

While Christ interspersed the *philia* and *agape* forms of love in this interchange, his goal was to acquire an answer regarding the highest form of love. Noteworthy in the passage is the call to action that follows Peter's positive responses. Christ does not respond with, "That's great, Peter. Thank you!" but instead propels him with lofty imperatives. Christ knew that his time was short and was, therefore, preparing Peter to take over the ministry of caring for Christ's elect. The dialogue between Christ and Peter provides a wonderful example of the necessity of *agape* love in Christian leadership. Peter was the de facto leader among the apostles and carried the responsibility of leading with love for the glory of God.

Although Christ's atoning death on the cross was his supreme act of love, his earthly ministry is replete with instances of actions which flow from genuine love. Before his arrest, Christ used his final moments in the upper room discourse to prepare his disciples and future leaders to love others by humbly serving them. He used one of the most humiliating examples to present this point by washing the apostles' feet. The Johannine account records, "Jesus, knowing that the Father had given all things into his hands, and that he had come from God and was going back to God, rose from supper. He laid aside his outer garments, and taking a towel, tied it around his waist. Then he poured water into a basin and began to wash

---

11. McKenzie, *Dictionary of the Bible*, 521.
12. John 21:15–17.

the disciples' feet and to wipe them with the towel that was wrapped around him."[13] Laney explains the cultural implications of this event:

> In Palestine the roads are dusty, and though guests would normally bathe before a social gathering like Passover, after a walk across the city their feet would be dirty. A basin of water and towels were customarily placed at the door of a home for washing. The task of washing guests' feet was generally assigned to a household servant. A basin of water and towel had been left in the upper room for the disciple's use, but not one of them had taken on the responsibility for washing the others' feet. They were too busy thinking of themselves to think of others.[14]

This event occurred at the feast of the Passover, where Christ was preparing for his arrest, torture, and execution. These incidents paint a picture of one who was headed into something more horrid than any other man would ever face, but cared more about preparing his disciples to love others in genuine humility. Christ used his final acts to reveal the supreme nature of *agape* love to his followers so they, in turn, would provide the example of Christ's love throughout the world and for future generations. Christ took on the role of a servant to illustrate how these future Christian leaders should lead.

As the Apostles would be the first to spread the gospel to various regions, they had to know it was based upon sacrificial, *agape* love. Following this act of love, Christ speaks:

> Do you understand what I have done to you? You call me Teacher and Lord, and you are right, for so I am. If I then, your Lord and Teacher, have washed your feet, you also ought to wash one another's feet. For I have given you an example, that you also should do just as I have done to you. Truly, truly, I say to you, a servant is not greater than his master, nor is a messenger greater than the one who sent him. If you know these things, blessed are you if you do them.[15]

In this instance, Christ, the Son of God and Creator of the universe (John 1:1–3), is condescending to set an example for all Christians, especially leaders, to follow. This servant model is countercultural to postmodernity as it asks for and requires nothing in return. Regarding this illustration by Christ, Gill notes:

---

13. John 13:3–5.
14. Laney, *John*, 239.
15. John 13:12–17.

> Christ is an example to his people, in many things; not in his miraculous performances and mediatorial work, but in the exercise of grace, of meekness, humility, love, patience, and the like; and in the discharge of duty, in submission to ordinances, and in attending on them; and in the several duties, both to them that are without, and to them that are within; and also in his sufferings and death; not that he died merely as an example, but likewise in the room and stead of his people; but here he is spoken of, as an example, in a particular instance.[16]

The totality of Christ's work provides an array of instances for Christian leaders to consider replicating. However, it is the heart of the labor and not necessarily the exact actions of Christ which one must emulate. For example, although the washing of the feet provided a view into how one might serve others, it is the love of the act and not the act itself which is efficacious.

Although the act of washing someone else's feet may be helpful, in contemporary culture its observance may not be readily understood nor appreciated. However, acts such as assisting disabled persons, visiting prisoners, or feeding those without means may provide service opportunities. Even these acts, accomplished with the wrong motives, such as "to be seen," are antithetical to biblical instruction, as God looks at the heart to determine sincerity of actions (1 Sam 16:7, Jer 17:10, Ps 26:2, Acts 8:22, Eph 6:6). For this reason, Christ often chastised the Pharisees for appearing righteous while simultaneously being corrupt on the inside (Matt 23:27). Christian leaders are, first and foremost, followers of Christ and servants of humanity, regardless of position, wealth, or authority. Although it is tempting for leaders to become arrogant when so much attention is given to them, Christian leaders must continually resist this, as pride is contrary to Christ's teaching. Leaders are charged with greater responsibilities than others; this can be used for good or for evil. Either way, leaders will be held to account for how they live out this God-given role (Jas 3:1, 1 Pet 4:5), for they are answerable for the souls in their care.

Just as a light bulb requires electricity to illuminate a room, humanity is unable to truly understand and live out *agape* love unless they are "plugged in" to its only source, Jesus Christ. Although those outside of the faith may exhibit "good" behavior, and may be very kind and giving people, their actions do not glorify God, as their source and motive is not in Christ. The Apostle John writes, "Beloved, let us love one another, for love is from

---

16. Gill, *Exposition*, para. 1.

God, and whoever loves has been born of God and knows God."[17] This verse presents a clear basis for genuine love, which is God himself. As he alone is the sole source of true love, one must be a part of him to embrace it and live it out in thought, word, and deed. Regarding this verse, Barnes provides clarification:

> Everyone who has true love to Christians as such, or true brotherly love, is a true Christian. This cannot mean that everyone that loves his wife and children, his classmate, his partner in business, or his friend—his house, or his farms, or his horses, or his hounds, is a child of God; it must be understood as referring to the point under discussion. A man may have a great deal of natural affection toward his kindred; a great amount of benevolence in his character toward the poor and needy, and still he may have none of the love to which John refers. He may have no real love to God, to the Saviour[sic], or to the children of God as such; and it would be absurd for such a one to argue because he loves his wife and children that therefore he loves God, or is born again.[18]

Barnes delineates between a general form of love and a genuine God-given *agape* love which manifests itself by the fruit of the Spirit in the believer's life to include "love, joy, peace, patience, kindness, goodness, faithfulness, gentleness, self-control."[19] For this reason, Scripture states they will be known "by their fruits."[20] If a leader is a regenerated believer in Christ, he will desire to lead in a way which honors Christ.

As postmodernity has provided an opportunity for the masses to redefine love in a variety of ways, the *eros* or *philia* forms of love have become more conducive to Hollywood culture. Postmodern society places a heavy emphasis on feelings and emotion over empiricism and facts, which were emphasized in the shift from modernity to postmodernity. This transition allowed something powerful to be redesigned into something destructive. One might think changing the definition of love has little bearing on the overall culture. However, considering the rapid transition away from traditional marriage and the commonplace nature of divorce in postmodern society, it is plausible that the redefinition of love played a large part due to its heavy emphasis on feelings over sacrifice and its focus on individuals

---

17. 1 John 4:7.
18. Barnes, "Section on 1 John 4:7."
19. Gal 5:22–23.
20. Matt 7:20.

rather than the Creator. When love becomes anything one wishes it to be, it becomes nothing worth pursuing. In his later epistle, the Apostle John presents a test for true love:

> By this we know love, that he laid down his life for us, and we ought to lay down our lives for the brothers. But if anyone has the world's goods and sees his brother in need, yet closes his heart against him, how does God's love abide in him? Little children, let us not love in word or talk but in deed and in truth.[21]

Again, this passage shows that true *agape* love is both sacrificial and service related, not a feeling or an emotion.

Even the most ardent of atheists holds to the concept of love, while denying its ultimate source. In a letter penned to his young daughter, author and renowned atheist Richard Dawkins writes,

> People sometimes say that you must believe in feelings deep inside, otherwise you'd never be confident of things like "My wife loves me." But this is a bad argument. There can be plenty of evidence that somebody loves you. All through the day when you are with somebody who loves you, you see and hear lots of little tidbits of evidence, and they all add up. It isn't purely inside feeling, like the feeling that priests call revelation. There are outside things to back up the inside feeling: looks in the eye, tender notes in the voice, little favors and kindnesses; this is all real evidence.[22]

Dawkins appears to comprehend the visual signs of love as real evidence but, oddly enough, is unable to explain its derivation. As a scientist, Dawkins prides himself on finding a scientific basis for all that exists. In the case of love, he presents evidence for something without an origin, defying accepted investigative scientific principles. In postmodernity, as with other terms, each person decides for himself how to define love. These postmodern definitions are mostly viewed through the lens of popular culture, which is largely based on what one can get from another person with a highly transactional emphasis. In other words, "I will love you if you love me." This highly emotional view of love uses feelings-based parameters to determine if one should be loved and under what circumstances that love should cease. This pluralistic and fluid view of love is radically different from love as presented by God in the Scriptures.

---

21. 1 John 3:16–18.
22. Dawkins, *A Devil's Chaplain*, 246.

In this Matthean pericope, Christ presents love without any qualifiers or conditions, while answering his agitators:

> But when the Pharisees heard that he had silenced the Sadducees, they gathered together. And one of them, a lawyer, asked him a question to test him. "Teacher, which is the great commandment in the Law?" And he said to him, "You shall love the Lord your God with all your heart and with all your soul and with all your mind. This is the great and first commandment. And a second is like it: You shall love your neighbor as yourself. On these two commandments depend all the Law and the Prophets.[23]

While the Pharisee would have concurred with the first commandment, the second one likely produced jeers. The Pharisees, while appearing to be the godliest people in the land, were not known for the kind treatment of others unless, of course, they were being watched. These two commandments reveal that we are to honor God first, and in doing so, we will love our neighbor. Christ provides no disclaimers on what kind of neighbor is to be loved, which means that everyone should be the recipient of such concern. Christ never commands his hearers to hate anyone, but instead compels the Christian to love even his enemy. As Matthew's gospel records:

> You have heard that it was said, "Love your neighbor and hate your enemy." But I tell you, love your enemies and pray for those who persecute you, that you may be children of your Father in heaven. He causes his sun to rise on the evil and the good, and sends rain on the righteous and the unrighteous. If you love those who love you, what reward will you get? Are not even the tax collectors doing that? And if you greet only your own people, what are you doing more than others? Do not even pagans do that? Be perfect, therefore, as your heavenly Father is perfect.[24]

Consequently, the Christian leader has one primary job in relation to his followers: to love them with the love of Christ with no conditions or strings attached. Although this task is easier said than done, Christian leaders, through the power of the Holy Spirit, are both equipped and commanded to do so. Also, as recipients of God's saving grace, each believer can appreciate the concept of loving the "unlovable" based on Christ's sacrifice for the souls of the wretched. When a Christian leader chooses to love his followers, he will be able to serve them by praying for them, listening to

---

23. Matt 22:34–40.
24. Matt 5:43–48 (NIV).

their concerns, treating them fairly, and providing a morally sound work environment. The Apostle John sums up these points well: "A new commandment I give to you, that you love one another: just as I have loved you, you also are to love one another. By this, all people will know that you are my disciples, if you have love for one another."[25]

---

25. John 13:34–35.

6

Reformational Leadership
Serving through the Solas

> *What distinguishes the arid ages from the period of the Reformation, when nations were moved as they had not been since Paul preached in Ephesus, Corinth, and Rome, is the latter's fullness of knowledge of God's Word. To echo an early Reformation thought, when the ploughman and the garage attendant know the Bible as well as the theologian does, and know it better than some contemporary theologians, then the desired awakening shall have already occurred.*
>
> —PROFESSOR GORDON H. CLARK[1]

THE PROTESTANT REFORMATION OF the sixteenth century ushered in a whole new era with its transformation (or reformation) of the Christian church. Reformers believed the church ventured so far off the intended scriptural path that it was no longer recognizable. Although the Reformation was replete with leaders in various countries pleading for change, three men stood as the primary representatives or leaders of the movement: Martin Luther, John Calvin, and Huldrych Zwingli. This triad, under the continual threat of persecution and execution, worked to reinstate biblical authority and inerrancy in the church while seeking to abolish the strict

---

1. Clark, *Historiography*.

hierarchy filled with political corruption and obligatory giving, known as indulgences. The demagogues who fought against these Reformers were eventually defeated, and a new age was born. John Calvin writes,

> But in promising it, of what sort did he declare his Spirit would be? One that would speak not from himself but would suggest to and instill into their minds what he had handed on through the Word (John 16:13). Therefore the Spirit, promised to us, has not the task of inventing new and unheard-of revelations, or of forging a new kind of doctrine, to lead us away from the received doctrine of the gospel, but of sealing our minds with that very doctrine which is commended by the gospel.[2]

Calvin and the other Reformers did not seek to construct a new church, philosophy, or doctrine, but instead sought to reestablish the original intent of Christ and the apostles as presented in the Bible.

The Reformation leaders exemplified the attributes of faith, grace, humility, courage, and boldness as they sought to correct the errors within the church, while encouraging the faithful to worship Christ in Spirit and in truth (John 4:24). This task was enormous, for the Roman Church at the time was considered the gateway for believers to have a relationship with God. This strict religious hierarchy allowed for considerable abuse, as clergy threatened congregants with an eternity in hell if they did not obey their instructions concerning indulgences and other matters. Although the Reformers were far from being a monolithic group, they did seek and find unity in a core set of biblical doctrines on which they would not budge. The codicil agreed upon by the Reformers are affectionately known as the "Five Solas." The Five Solas were designed to ensure that, whateverelse may be disputed, these five principles should never be tampered with nor revised. Each of the *solas* are formed from their Latin origin, which provided a central focus for each doctrine. These include *Sola Fide* (faith alone), *Sola Scriptura* (Scripture alone), *Solus Christus* (Christ alone), *Sola Gratia* (grace alone), and *Soli Deo Gloria* (glory to God alone). The following summary of the Five Solas is presented in the modern restatement of *The Cambridge Declaration of the Alliance of Confessing Evangelicals*:

- Faith Alone (*Sola Fide*)

    Justification is by grace alone through faith alone because of Christ alone. In justification Christ's righteousness is imputed to us as the

---

2. Calvin, *Institutes*, 94.

only possible satisfaction of God's perfect justice. Our justification does not rest on any merit to be found in us, nor upon the grounds of an infusion of Christ's righteousness in us, nor that an institution claiming to be a church that denies or condemns sola fide can be recognized as a legitimate church.

- Scripture Alone (*Sola Scriptura*)

    The inerrant Scripture (the Bible) is the sole source of written divine revelation, which alone can bind the conscience. The Bible alone teaches all that is necessary for our salvation from sin and is the standard by which all Christian behavior must be measured. It is denied that any creed, council or individual may bind a Christian's conscience, that the Holy Spirit speaks independently of or contrary to what is set forth in the Bible, or that personal spiritual experience can ever be a vehicle of revelation.

- Christ Alone (*Solus Christus*)

    Our salvation is accomplished by the mediatorial work of the historical Christ alone. His sinless life and substitutionary atonement alone are sufficient for our justification and reconciliation to the Father. It is denied that the gospel is preached if Christ's substitutionary work is not declared and faith in Christ and his work is not solicited.

- Grace Alone (*Sola Gratia*)

    In salvation we are rescued from God's wrath by his grace alone. It is the supernatural work of the Holy Spirit that brings us to Christ by releasing us from our bondage to sin and raising us from spiritual death to spiritual life. It is denied that salvation is in any sense a human work. Human methods, techniques or strategies by themselves cannot accomplish this transformation. Faith is not produced by our unregenerated human nature.

- Glory to God Alone (*Soli Deo Gloria*)

    It is affirmed that because salvation is of God and has been accomplished by God, it is for God's glory and that we must glorify him always. We must live our entire lives before the face of God, under the authority of God and for his glory alone. It is denied that we can properly glorify God if our worship is confused with entertainment, if we neglect either Law or Gospel in our preaching, or if self-improvement, self-esteem or self-fulfillment are allowed to become alternatives to the gospel.[3]

It may cause some to wonder how a manuscript on the topic of leadership relates to the Five Solas of the Reformation. As each of the *solas* are considered, the Christian leader has five core principles from which to lead. Leading according to the principles of Scripture, through Christ's teachings and examples, in a gracious manner, by faith, and for God's glory alone provide an exemplary groundwork from which to develop Christian leadership theory. Just as the Reformers labored to ensure their core principles for the Christian church were accurate, so should every Christian leader, regardless of the environment. To lead wisely, one needs to understand the source of wisdom as provided in the Scriptures.

When King Solomon was given the opportunity to request anything he wished, he pursued wisdom to lead his people. Consider the following discourse between God and Solomon:

> In that night God appeared to Solomon, and said to him, "Ask what I shall give you." And Solomon said to God, "You have shown great and steadfast love to David my father, and have made me king in his place. O Lord God, let your word to David my father be now fulfilled, for you have made me king over a people as numerous as the dust of the earth. Give me now wisdom and knowledge to go out and come in before this people, for who can govern this people of yours, which is so great?" God answered Solomon, "Because this was in your heart, and you have not asked for possessions, wealth, honor, or the life of those who hate you, and have not even asked for long life, but have asked for wisdom and knowledge for yourself that you may govern my people over whom I have made you king, wisdom and knowledge are granted to you. I will also give you riches, possessions, and honor, such as none of the kings had who were before you, and none after you shall have the like." So Solomon came from the high place at Gibeon, from before the tent of meeting, to Jerusalem. And he reigned over Israel.[4]

With the ability to ask for anything that he wished from God, Solomon requested the ability to govern his people with wisdom. Although this pericope is not designed as a template for each person to get one wish from God, it does make the strong point that wisdom in leadership should be

---

3. Alliance of Confessing Evangelicals, *The Cambridge Declaration*.
4. 2 Chr 1:7–13.

pursued with vigor. Wisdom, outside of its descriptions throughout the Bible, is a nebulous term, very open to one's own definition. Therefore, Christian leaders can only know true wisdom from continual study of God's word. The Apostle Paul proclaims, "All Scripture is breathed out by God and profitable for teaching, for reproof, for correction, and for training in righteousness, that the man of God may be complete, equipped for every good work."[5] While the options for books on leadership are abundant, the greatest source is that which was given by God himself.

Leading Sola Fide

The word *faith* conjures up a multitude of meanings, as some consider it in the following ways: "I have faith this chair will hold me," "I have faith we will win our game," "I have faith in my doctor," "I have faith in humanity," or "I have faith my car will get me to work today." Each of these aspects of faith are based more on hope than faith as the chair leg may break, the game may be lost, my doctor may give the wrong medicine, humanity may produce acts of terrorism, and the car may blow a tire. While the word *faith* is ubiquitous in postmodern culture, like all other terms, it is defined by the beholder. The Scriptures provide the context for faith as something much more substantive than simply wishing for something to come true. Like the aforementioned topic of love, faith is often confused with feelings, and like love, action is always predicated on faith. Hebrews chapter eleven is often called the "Hall of Faith," as it defines faith and then chronicles the faith of many saints by their deeds. The author of Hebrews writes,

> Now faith is the assurance of things hoped for, the conviction of things not seen. For by it the people of old received their commendation. By faith we understand that the universe was created by the word of God, so that what is seen was not made out of things that are visible. By faith Abel offered to God a more acceptable sacrifice than Cain, through which he was commended as righteous, God commending him by accepting his gifts. And through his faith, though he died, he still speaks. By faith Enoch was taken up so that he should not see death, and he was not found, because God had taken him. Now before he was taken he was commended as having pleased God. And without faith it is impossible to please him, for whoever would draw near to God must believe that he exists and that he rewards those who seek him. By faith Noah,

---

5. 2 Tim 3:16–17.

being warned by God concerning events as yet unseen, in reverent fear constructed an ark for the saving of his household. By this he condemned the world and became an heir of the righteousness that comes by faith.[6]

Faith, as described by the author of Hebrews, results in "assurance" and "conviction" and is honored by God as righteous thoughts and behaviors. Having faith that God created the universe is beyond believing that it was "very likely," but instead, faith is concrete, "knowing" that he created all that exists. As seen by the examples of Abel, Enoch, Noah, and the rest, faith produced action in each occasion. If one has faith in God, he will follow God because he "knows" who God is and what he desires. Johnstone posits, "Faith is knowledge based, and this knowledge comes from the Bible: *So then faith cometh by hearing, and hearing by the word of God.* (Rom 10:17)."[7] Therefore, it is our responsibility to take what God has declared and to proclaim it. We should always remember that one of the hallmarks of the Reformation was a resurgence of the centrality of Bible preaching.[8] Faith based on knowledge, truth, conviction, and assurance leads to humility, grace, and action. This glorifies God and is commended by him. Regarding the Hebrews passage, theologian John Brown writes:

> The apostle now, for the illustration and enforcement of his exhortation, brings forth a great variety of instances, from the history of former ages, in which faith had enabled individuals to perform very difficult duties, endure very severe trials, and obtain very important blessings. The principles of the apostle's exhortation are plainly these: "They who turn back, turn back into perdition. It is only they who persevere in believing that obtain the salvation of the soul. Nothing but a persevering faith can enable a person, through a constant continuance in well-doing, and a patient, humble submission to the will of God, to obtain that glory, honour[sic], and immortality which the gospel promises. Nothing but a persevering faith can do it, as is plain from what it has done in the former ages."[9]

Not only does faith result in actions which glorify God, but it also provides perseverance to the believer. Faith in Christ, while necessary to attain salvation, does not end at the time when the soul is first regenerated; it

---

6. Heb 11:1–7.
7. Free Presbyterian Church, "Why Do the Five Solas Matter Today?"
8. Ibid.
9. Brown, *Hebrews*, 487–88.

only begins the journey. As Christian leaders are tested, they grow through the process of sanctification. As they grow, they also develop perseverance to better prepare them for the next trial. Consequently, each challenge further strengthens the Christian leader in persevering. Consider the Apostle Paul's words regarding the impact of faith:

> Therefore, since we have been justified by faith, we have peace with God through our Lord Jesus Christ. Through him we have also obtained access by faith into this grace in which we stand, and we rejoice in hope of the glory of God. Not only that, but we rejoice in our sufferings, knowing that suffering produces endurance, and endurance produces character, and character produces hope, and hope does not put us to shame, because God's love has been poured into our hearts through the Holy Spirit who has been given to us.[10]

This passage presents some powerful truth regarding faith. First, faith is the basis of justification; Christ is taking the believer's sins upon himself and filling him with the righteousness of God. Second, faith provides full and unhindered access to God. The Old Covenant required animal sacrifices for the covering of sin which was temporal and needed to be frequently accomplished. Also, the Old Testament saints relied on the high priest to access the place of God, or the "Holy of Holies." Through faith, every Christian has direct access to God without the need of priests or deceased saints. Finally, faith takes the believer from suffering to endurance to character to hope.

An argument can be made that everyone has faith. While this faith may be in one's self, another person, an object, or a religious figure, everyone puts his life's focus on something and acts in a way to serve that object of affection. Jesus provided this warning:

> Do not lay up for yourselves treasures on earth, where moth and rust destroy and where thieves break in and steal, but lay up for yourselves treasures in heaven, where neither moth nor rust destroys and where thieves do not break in and steal. For where your treasure is, there your heart will be also.[11]

The treasure Jesus was referring to in this passage was the object of faith in one's life. Christ's imperative exhorted the hearers to place their faith in that which is eternal, as everything else will one day cease to exist.

---

10. Rom 5:1–5.
11. Matt 6:19–21.

Christian leaders must be people of faith, faith in the God who created them and gifted them to serve in leadership. While the treasures of this world are a constant temptation, leaders must maintain a centrality of focus to refrain from leading others astray, while providing a useful example of true and saving faith.

Anyone who has served in a leadership capacity for any amount of time can testify that conflict and uncertainty are often present. While it may seem easy to have strong faith during times of peace and success, it is during trials when faith is tested the most. Christian leaders are blessed to have the Holy Spirit within them to drive them closer to Christ, and trials are God's means for this to occur. While reading of the trials of Job, the persecution of Daniel, and the execution of Stephen, the Christian leader can take solace in knowing God will never abandon him nor forsake him in his darkest moments. The Christian leader can hold firmly to the promise of God that he will never leave nor forsake his own (Deut 31:6, Heb 13:5). Under the severest hardships, leaders often feel alone and disregarded. During these times, their faith becomes stronger as they are carried through the fire, just as Shadrach, Meshach, and Abednego were spared by God in the furnace (Dan 3:16–28). Engstrom notes:

> Leadership is lonely! [A leader] may be ignored or even betrayed by people he felt he could count on. Spiritual faith is a demand even when the objectives are material or secular in nature. The fruit of strong faith is a serenity that rises above the turmoil and provides balance when the leader must stand against many odds. These are essential for a successful leader. Without them, discouragement and despair can easily set in.[12]

Faith, therefore, provides excellent comfort for Christian leaders struggling with hardships as they always have the guidance of the counselor and comforter, namely the Holy Spirit, to see them through.

Faith also reveals a genuineness to a Christian leader's belief system. Anyone can claim to be a Christian (and most in America do), but it is rare to find people truly living out the Christian faith in thought, word, and deed. As discussed previously, faith must lead to actions, and if the focus of the faith is Jesus Christ, the behavior must emulate his character through good works. Although Scripture is clear that one is not saved by good works (Eph 2:9), it is just as apparent that works are a necessary by-product of salvation. In his epistle, James writes:

---

12. Engstrom, *Making of a Christian Leader*, 37.

> What good is it, my brothers, if someone says he has faith but does not have works? Can that faith save him? If a brother or sister is poorly clothed and lacking in daily food, and one of you says to them, "Go in peace, be warmed and filled," without giving them the things needed for the body, what good is that? So also faith by itself, if it does not have works, is dead. But someone will say, "You have faith and I have works." Show me your faith apart from your works, and I will show you my faith by my works.[13]

James presents a compelling argument for faith being a precursor to good works. The Christian leader has a moral obligation to meet the needs of his followers if it is in his ability to do so. Furthermore, in meeting this need, he is illustrating the love of Christ, as exemplified in the Savior's servant leadership.

Leading Sola Sciptura

As evidenced by the overabundance of books about leadership, it is apparent that leaders are eagerly seeking a framework by which to lead others. Although reading from multiple vantage points is useful in understanding the breadth of leadership theories, only one source provides indisputable answers to the questions which leaders seek: the Holy Bible. Although the Scriptures have many critics, the truths contained within have stood the test of thousands of years of scrutiny by the most educated skeptics. It was the Reformation Era which revived the attributes of inerrancy, infallibility, sufficiency, authority, and perspicuity of Scripture. The Reformers also furthered the cause of their predecessors John Wycliffe, John Hus, and Johann Gutenberg by translating the Bible into each region's native language. No longer were Christian services to be limited to Latin, an unfamiliar language to most hearers. Copies of the text eventually became plentiful for the layman, allowing one to be able to study the Scriptures for himself. This new world encouraged a personal relationship with Christ, outside of the need for priests and popes, and was open to everyone. By raising the prominence of the Scriptures, people had the opportunity to test for themselves that which is true (1 Thess 5:21). According to the Westminster Confession, "The supreme judge by which all controversies of religion are to be determined, and all decrees of councils, opinions of ancient writers, doctrines of men, and private spirits, are to be examined, and in whose sentence we

---

13. Jas 2:14–18.

are to rest, can be no other but the Holy Spirit speaking in the Scripture."[14] When divine truth was elevated, people were given an objective standard by which to compare everything else. Writing for the Presbyterian Record, James Thomson notes:

> Scripture alone—this has been one of the ringing proclamations upon which the Protestant world has built the basis of its understanding of the Christian faith. The 66 books of the Old and New Testaments recognized by Protestants have been understood to be the rule of faith and life—not church councils or ancient creeds, not pronouncements of bishops or conclaves. Through the guidance of the Holy Spirit, the Bible is to be interpreted by reference to itself. It is the witness of the whole canon and not bits and pieces chosen at random that opens to us our understanding of God.[15]

Consequently, as a priest or pastor preached a sermon, the common man could study to see if his teachings aligned with the Bible. Prior to this time, the congregation was required to place blind faith and trust in their clergies and assume that they spoke for God and without error. Thomson continues:

> When Luther and other Reformers demanded that the Bible be made available to the laity in their own language, they firmly believed that these inspired Scriptures, under the guidance of the Holy Spirit and the leadership of Reformed theologians, would break Christians free from the authority of the medieval church with its suspect practices, such as the use of indulgences for the remission of sins.[16]

Thus, the faithful were provided a strong element of protection from false teachings and false teachers who would no longer be able to fool the laypeople with deceptive practices.

As Christian leaders, it is tempting to grab the most recent leadership book written by a nationally renowned guru for assistance in organizational decision making. Although opening the mind to new ideas and theories can be beneficial, having something tangible and concrete to compare extrabiblical writings against aids in the discernment process. While a secular author may present some excellent insights for a leader to consider, holding the book up to the light of Scripture can help in separating truth from error or wisdom from foolishness. Also, the Scriptures are replete with examples

---

14. Williamson, *Westminster*, 31.
15. Thomson, "Sola Scriptura," 17–18.
16. Ibid.

of leadership to emulate. From David, Solomon, and Nehemiah to Peter, Paul, and John, each Old and New Testament model provides a wealth of material to study in the field of leadership. As the lives of biblical leaders are investigated, the evidence reveals that they were all ordinary, sinful men with challenges no different than any others, but were called of God to lead people through very difficult times. These case studies show their failures, successes, and ultimate dependence upon God in leading and loving others. The men were not only called by God to lead, but they were equipped by him to do so for his glory. Another commonality amongst these leaders is that they all held firmly to the sacred text of their time, primarily Old Testament manuscripts or words from God's prophets, which would later be added to the canon of Scripture.

Each Bible leader also grew in faith through conflict, which gives encouragement to every contemporary leader facing similar challenges. The Apostle Paul willingly traveled over ten thousand miles from country to country on land and sea, facing bandits and persecution for the sole purpose of spreading the gospel. The following Pauline narrative provides a powerful depiction of a person transformed by the gospel and willing to sacrifice everything to ensure others hear it:

> Five times I received at the hands of the Jews the forty lashes less one. Three times I was beaten with rods. Once I was stoned. Three times I was shipwrecked; a night and a day I was adrift at sea; on frequent journeys, in danger from rivers, danger from robbers, danger from my own people, danger from Gentiles, danger in the city, danger in the wilderness, danger at sea, danger from false brothers; in toil and hardship, through many a sleepless night, in hunger and thirst, often without food, in cold and exposure. And, apart from other things, there is the daily pressure on me of my anxiety for all the churches. Who is weak, and I am not weak? Who is made to fall, and I am not indignant? If I must boast, I will boast of the things that show my weakness. The God and Father of the Lord Jesus, he who is blessed forever, knows that I am not lying.[17]

Paul, knowing that each journey would be likely filled with peril, continued on without hesitation, knowing that his cause was just and that his God would see him through. What a perfect example of genuine love, faith, and an unwavering pursuit of truth amid incessant storms. This and many other

---

17. 2 Cor 11:24–31.

biblical accounts should embolden leaders to pursue their callings with passion and courage.

Leading Solus Christus

In the past decade, numerous books have been written about the purpose of one's life. Although many answers are available for those seeking to understand their human existences (family, friends, church, missions, vocation, and evangelism), each of these is only a part of a much larger response for the Christian. The Westminster Shorter Catechism provides concise questions and answers regarding the purpose for humanity's existence with the supporting proof texts:

Q: What is the chief end of man?

A: Man's chief end is to glorify God, and to enjoy him forever.

- Whether therefore ye eat, or drink, or whatsoever ye do, do all to the glory of God.[18]
- For of him, and through him, and to him, are all things: to whom be glory for ever. Amen.[19]
- Thou shalt guide me with thy counsel, and afterward receive me to glory. Whom have I in heaven but thee? and there is none upon earth that I desire beside thee. My flesh and my heart faileth: but God is the strength of my heart, and my portion for ever.[20]
- And the glory which thou gavest me I have given them; that they may be one, even as we are one . . . Father, I will that they also, whom thou hast given me, be with me where I am; that they may behold my glory, which thou hast given me: for thou lovedst me before the foundation of the world.[21, 22]

---

18. 1 Cor 10:31 (KJV).
19. Rom 11:36 (KJV).
20. Ps 73:24–26 (KJV).
21. John 17:22, 24 (KJV).
22. *The Westminster Shorter Catechism*, 1.

The Westminster Divines, who worked diligently to produce the Westminster Confession and Catechism as a tool to instruct believers in the essentials of the Christian faith, were unashamedly christocentric in their labors. While the question of man's purpose has been debated by philosophers and others for centuries, the Divines provided a succinct and unambiguous response to this age-old question with a simple two-part response: to glorify and enjoy him forever. The "God" and the "him" in the reply is Jesus Christ, who is one with the Father and the Holy Spirit, comprising the Blessed Trinity.

In postmodernity, the tendency toward spirituality involves syncretism, or an amalgam of gods or ideas about God which comprises one's system of belief. An example is combining the servant nature of Jesus with the desire for Nirvana, while disregarding any eschatological judgment for sin. Postmodernists feel free to create the god of their choosing by combining what they prefer about each religion, thereby creating something designed to make them feel better about their existences. Beeke writes:

> We urgently need to hear *Solus Christus* in our day of pluralistic theology. Many people today question the belief that salvation is only by faith in Christ. As Carl Braaten says, they "are returning to a form of the old bankrupt nineteenth-century Christological approach of Protestant liberalism and calling it 'new,' when it is actually scarcely more than a shallow Jesusology." The end result is that today, many people—as H. R. Niebuhr famously said of liberalism—proclaim and worship "a God without wrath who brought men without sin into a kingdom without judgment through the ministrations of a Christ without a cross."[23]

Solus Christus presents Christ as "God alone," without the ability to add or detract.

The claims of Christ's exclusivity were not a latter-day doctrinal development, but were proclaimed by Christ himself in the Gospel of John:

> "Let not your hearts be troubled. Believe in God; believe also in me. In my Father's house are many rooms. If it were not so, would I have told you that I go to prepare a place for you? And if I go and prepare a place for you, I will come again and will take you to myself, that where I am you may be also. And you know the way to where I am going." Thomas said to him, "Lord, we do not know where you are going. How can we know the way?" Jesus said to him, "I am the way, and the truth, and the life. No one comes to the Father except through me. If you had known me, you would

---

23. Beeke, "Christ Alone." para. 4.

have known my Father also. From now on you do know him and have seen him."[24]

Few dispute that Christ uttered these words, and even less would find them to be difficult to interpret. Christ is saying very pointedly, "I am God, and no other plan of salvation exists outside of me." The challenge for every person hearing the claims of Christ is how to respond.

Christian leaders, if they are living according to their callings, are leading *Solus Christus* or "for Christ alone." Although Christians should plan, pursue, and pray for God's will in their vocations, their foremost emphases should be glorifying Christ. Some questions for Christian leaders to ask regarding their pursuits include the following:

- Am I living a life which reflects the work of Christ in my life?
- Do I seek Christ's will first in leading others or is it more often an afterthought?
- Am I willing to leave my vocation if it requires me to renounce my love for and calling from Christ?
- Do I seek to put others before myself in humility as modeled by Christ?
- Do others see Christ in me?
- Am I in continual repentance for my sin based on Christ's atoning work?
- Am I ashamed to share Christ with others?
- Am I willing to share of the gospel of Christ with those around me regardless of the potential consequences?
- Are my actions and words in harmony as they relate to my Christian testimony?
- Will I defend truth even if the consequences are severe?
- Would I sacrifice everything for the cause of Christ?

The sole purpose of Christian leadership is to glorify the Savior in all aspects of life and to live by faith as an example to those watching or willing to listen.

---

24. John 14:1–7.

Leading Sola Gratia

The next facet of Reformational Leadership involves a commonly misunderstood term: grace, under its Latin name *gratia*. Grace is seldom discussed in the realm of leadership theory, as it solely involves the act of giving, without the prospect of something in return. *Sola gratia* is translated as "by grace alone" and carries the belief that Christians are saved by grace alone (not works), according to Scripture. As explained earlier, works are a byproduct of redemption and not the causation. Though the Roman Church adopted the doctrine of works, the Reformers sought guidance through God's word, particularly the Pauline epistles, in which it is abundantly clear that it is only by God's grace that one is saved. In clarifying this point to the church in Ephesus, the Apostle Paul encouraged the faithful with the following:

> And you were dead in the trespasses and sins in which you once walked, following the course of this world, following the prince of the power of the air, the spirit that is now at work in the sons of disobedience—among whom we all once lived in the passions of our flesh, carrying out the desires of the body and the mind, and were by nature children of wrath, like the rest of mankind. But God, being rich in mercy, because of the great love with which he loved us, even when we were dead in our trespasses, made us alive together with Christ—by grace you have been saved—and raised us up with him and seated us with him in the heavenly places in Christ Jesus, so that in the coming ages he might show the immeasurable riches of his grace in kindness toward us in Christ Jesus. For by grace you have been saved through faith. And this is not your own doing; it is the gift of God, not a result of works, so that no one may boast. For we are his workmanship, created in Christ Jesus for good works, which God prepared beforehand, that we should walk in them.[25]

Paul places the work of salvation exclusively on the person of Jesus Christ, and in doing so, reveals that all men are sinners (children of wrath) outside of Christ's intervention in regeneration. The *ordo salutis (order of salvation)* begins and ends with Jesus Christ from grace to glory. Paul also writes, "And I am sure of this, that he who began a good work in you will bring it to completion at the day of Jesus Christ" (Phil 1:6). The "good works" mentioned in this pericope involves forgiving others, just as forgiveness has been freely given by God. Grace, then, is unmerited favor by God

---

25. Eph 2:1–10.

to those whom he chooses (Eph 1) or, as Terry Johnson points out, "Grace, by definition, is that which is not required but given freely anyway ... grace is the un-required, un-obligated, self-determined, self-motivated, freely given mercy of God in Christ."[26] Grace is the most important gift one can receive, as it cannot be purchased or earned. For this reason, the Reformers worked diligently to revive this apostolic doctrine which had been maligned through the past centuries. *Amazing Grace*, the familiar hymn penned by John Newton in 1779, beautifully illustrates God's saving grace:

> Amazing Grace, how sweet the sound
> That saved a wretch like me!
> I once was lost, but now am found,
> Was blind, but now I see.
>
> 'Twas grace that taught my heart to fear,
> And grace my fears relieved.
> How precious did that grace appear
> The hour I first believed!
>
> Through many dangers, toils, and snares,
> I have already come.
> 'Tis grace hath brought me safe thus far,
> And grace will lead me home.
>
> And when this flesh and heart shall fail,
> And mortal life shall cease,
> I shall possess within the veil
> A life of joy and peace.
>
> When we've been there ten thousand years,
> Bright shining as the sun,
> We've no less days to sing God's praise
> Than when we first begun.

Christian leaders should strongly consider this selfless, giving act of grace in their pursuits of godliness. Although human leaders are not able to "save souls," they can be gracious in many other ways, primarily by offering

---

26. Johnson, *The Case for Traditional Protestantism*, 111.

forgiveness. In God's supreme act of grace, he forgives all past, present, and future sin, without qualification. Christian leaders, seeking to emulate Christ, must be willing to forgive followers in the same vein and be willing to suffer quietly for wrongs against them. Philip Hughes posits, "Indeed, the abject weakness of the human instrument serves to magnify and throw into relief the perfection of the divine power in a way that any suggestion of human adequacy could never do. The greater the servant's weakness, the more conspicuous is the power of his Master's all-sufficient grace."[27] Christian leaders are strong when weak and gracious, when they come to understand their own inadequacy. It is hard to be unforgiving to others when one considers the great amount of sin against a Holy God from whom they have been forgiven. When a leader continually forgives, he is setting the example for others to do likewise. Conversely, leaders who choose a path of resentment and retaliation can expect the same in return, as they are setting this tone for others to emulate. Leading by grace is not an easy task, for it requires sacrifice, humility, and selflessness, even at times when one wrongs the leader with intent and malice. However, the remembrance of Christ's grace in forgiveness should be a powerful motivator to do the same to others.

Leading Soli Deo Gloria

The quintessential goal of Christian leadership is to glorify God. This final *"sola"* encapsulates the others as the Christian leads by Scripture alone (the foundational source for the knowledge of God and his will), by faith alone (it is only by faith that man can please God), by Christ alone (honoring and following the one who was sacrificed for man's redemption), and by grace alone (the only way to mirror this powerful and humble attribute of God). Leading for the glory of God alone places the fullness of the Godhead in the position of supremacy in every word, act, and deed with the visceral purpose of loving him and desiring others to love him also. Johnstone notes, "The previous four solas logically lead us to 'Soli Deo Gloria' or the Glory of God Alone! Psalm 19:1 reminds us that God displays His glory in creation: *'The heavens declare the glory of God.'* Just as the moon reflects the light of the sun, the Christian should reflect the glory of God. This should be the desire, objective, and purpose of a Christian."[28] A leader sets the example to his followers by exemplifying the primacy of God's grace. If a leader fails

---

27. Hughes, *Second Corinthians*, 451.
28. Free Presbyterian Church, "Why Do the Five Solas Matter Today?", 22.

to lead wisely or falls into gross sin, observant unbelievers will question the leader's faith and the legitimacy of his God.

Glorifying God alone also means that nothing else becomes the primary focus for the believing leader. Hence, his desires, plans, intentions, goals, and actions involve Christlike-ness through servant leadership. In *A Body of Divinity*, Puritan Thomas Watson deals with the question presented earlier, "What is the chief end of man?" and answers with the following:

> We aim purely at His glory preferring God's glory above all other things. We glorify God by an ingenious confession of sin, by believing, by being tender of His glory, by fruitfulness, by being contented in the state in which Providence has placed us, by working out our own salvation, by living to God, by walking cheerfully, by standing up for his truth, by praising him, by being zealous for his name, when we have an eye to God in our natural and in our civil actions, by labouring to draw others to God; by seeking to convert others, and so make them instruments of glorifying God. We glorify God in a high degree when we suffer for God, and seal the gospel with our blood, when we give God the glory of all that we do, by a holy life.[29]

Watson aptly presents the many facets of glorifying God in our lives with not a single mention of self-awareness, self-esteem, selfish desires or any other aspect of self-elevation which would put us in competition with God. A Christian leader who desires to live *Soli Deo Gloria* is one who is unashamed of the Gospel and is willing to sacrifice everything for the glory of God. Christ, after foretelling his death to the disciples, explains in the severest of warnings that being a Christian means loving the Lord at all costs and forsaking the world and its allurements:

> And he said to all, "If anyone would come after me, let him deny himself and take up his cross daily and follow me. For whoever would save his life will lose it, but whoever loses his life for my sake will save it. For what does it profit a man if he gains the whole world and loses or forfeits himself? For whoever is ashamed of me and of my words, of him will the Son of Man be ashamed when he comes in his glory and the glory of the Father and of the holy angels.[30]

---

29. Watson and Reilly, *A Body of Divinity*, 10–18.
30. Luke 9:23–26.

The Leadership Imperative

Leading by faith alone, through grace alone, in Christ alone, by his word alone, for the glory of God alone, is the highest calling and greatest reward for the Christian leader.

7

Leading Change in a Culture of Fluidity

> *Interruption, incoherence, surprise are the ordinary conditions of our life. They have even become real needs for many people, whose minds are no longer fed . . . by anything but sudden changes and constantly renewed stimuli . . . We can no longer bear anything that lasts. We no longer know how to make boredom bear fruit. So the whole question comes down to this: can the human mind master what the human mind has made?*
>
> —PAUL VALERY[1]

TODAY'S WORLD IS CHANGING at a pace like never before in history, with the rapid growth and transformation of technology, global competition, and a redefining of traditional values. The world is also very small, in the sense that one can hit a button on a smartphone or computer and quickly speak face-to-face with someone in another country. The internet reveals formerly protected "secrets" of the world for all to see, and news travels from coast to coast in mere seconds. One might think that, by having a mountain of knowledge a few clicks away, humanity could solve any problem or properly handle change when it arises. Unfortunately, the busyness of the world has created significant challenges for leaders who wish to grow a disciplined, loyal, and focused workforce, as each of these attributes has been heavily plundered in

---

1. Bauman, "Foreword."

postmodernity. Change, however, is not new; it is simply manifesting itself in a way that is hard to manage. As Voehl and Harrington note,

> Some of the earliest writings of mankind were centered on change. Dating back as early as 3000 BCE, the *I Ching* or *Book of Changes* conceived the notion of change as inevitable, and resistance to change as one of humankind's greatest causes of pain. These early agents of change wrote that in order to affect change in a positive way, a balance was required between internal and external forces. But it is one thing to produce a momentary change and quite another to sustain that change.[2]

Voehl and Harrington's assessment regarding the inevitability of change, along with its internal and external forces, are still applicable today. The forces of change are always in motion, making the idea of status quo, as a leadership concept, untenable. In postmodernity, leaders must prepare themselves for new types of followers and be flexible enough to lead them through change. G. K. Chesterton uniquely explains this postmodernistic culture of fluidity:

> The real trouble with this world of ours is not that it is an unreasonable world, or even that it is a reasonable one. The commonest kind of the trouble is that it is nearly reasonable, but not quite. Life is not an illogicality, yet it is a trap for logicians. It looks just a little more mathematical and regular than it is; its exactitude is obvious, but its inexactitude is hidden; its wildness lies in wait.[3]

With the world in flux and constant change unavoidable, leading is not a task for the faint of heart. Each day presents new chaos, new ideas, new solutions, and new calamities which must be considered, researched, and decided upon. Leaders must seek to understand the world and its people to meet them where they are and guide them through life's changes. According to Fullan:

> Change is a double-edged sword, its relentless pace these days runs us off of our feet. Yet when things are unsettled, we can find new ways to move ahead and to create breakthroughs not possible in stagnant societies. If you ask people to brainstorm words to describe change, they come up with a mixture of negative and positive terms. On the one side, fear, anxiety, loss, danger, panic; on the other, exhilaration, risk-taking, excitement, improvements,

---

2. Voehl and Harrington, *Change Management*, 13.
3. Fullan, *Culture of Change*, xiii.

energizing. For better or for worse, change arouses emotions, and when emotions intensify, leadership is key.[4]

Change, therefore, can produce either fear or joy based on the impact of the change process. Due to the volatile nature of change, leaders must approach it with solemnity and handle it with care.

As change has been one of the few constants in the world, the Bible is replete with examples of monumental change. In fact, it can be argued that each time God intervened directly with humanity, tremendous changes occurred. The Apostle Paul became a powerful agent of change after his life was radically and instantly transformed by God. Paul led every change with empathy toward his hearers, knowing that trust must be established before the words of change could be accepted. Paul understood the need to know his audience and even become like them, if necessary, to reach them with divine truth (transformational change). In his letter to the church in Corinth, he explains how to reach others:

> For though I am free from all, I have made myself a servant to all, that I might win more of them. To the Jews I became as a Jew, in order to win Jews. To those under the law I became as one under the law (though not being myself under the law) that I might win those under the law. To those outside the law I became as one outside the law (not being outside the law of God but under the law of Christ) that I might win those outside the law. To the weak I became weak, that I might win the weak. I have become all things to all people, that by all means I might save some. I do it all for the sake of the gospel, that I may share with them in its blessings.[5]

Paul never compromised his faith or condoned acting like a "sinner" to reach unbelievers, but instead displayed the need for empathy so that the message would not be hindered. In postmodernity, a Christian leader should not sacrifice his deeply held convictions; instead, he should understand those with different values in order to develop a relationship of trust.

In leading an organization or any other group through a change process, the element of trust is key. Change can produce uncertainty, anger, distrust, insecurity, and stress if not managed properly. People feel most comfortable when things are steady and disruptions are at a minimum, but life rarely allows much time for periods of stability. During times of uncertainty, people are looking for a steady person to guide them through

4. Ibid., xiii.
5. 1 Cor 9:19–23.

the change. The change may be familial, such as the announcement of a diagnosis of cancer for a loved one, or the change may be organizational, with the threat of downsizing and layoffs. These types of changes catch people off guard and can be quite emotional. Christian leaders must be empathetic to those facing the reality of change that they may provide wise counsel, comfort, and prayer. Considering the need to lead *Soli Deo Gloria*, Christian leaders have much to offer those dealing with change—most importantly, the words of Christ, such as "I have said these things to you, that in me you may have peace. In the world, you will have tribulation. But take heart; I have overcome the world."[6] In this passage, Christ acknowledges that humans will go through trials in this life, but he also provides the good news that he has overcome the world. In following Christ, the believer also overcomes the world and has a future home in glory. This word of encouragement aids those facing life's challenges by providing an answer much greater than their temporary circumstance. Hence, no matter how bad it gets, Christ provides the greatest gift of all in the hope of glory.

Leaders must provide practical, wise counsel aligned with biblical principles to guide someone, or some entity, through the process of change. Change management is mostly discussed in the realm of leadership or management theory, for organizations either succeed or fail by how they manage change. Leaders have many tools available to guide them through unplanned changes, as well as the ability to create a culture of change which can prepare organizations for the next transformation. Forlaron writes:

> Change is now an ever-present feature of organizational life, at both an operational and strategic level. Managers must realize that one cannot separate strategic change management from organizational strategy; both must work in tandem. The importance of the human side of change cannot be underestimated; one must identify and manage the potential sources and causes of potential resistance and ensure that "motivators" are built into new processes and structures.[7]

This assessment demonstrates that the change process must be synergistic and bring in many voices to manage the issues at hand. One key element of change which leaders must never forget is that change impacts people's lives. While a manager may focus on cutting costs and building revenue, he should always consider how individuals' lives and the lives of their families

---

6. John 16:33.
7. Forlaron, "The Human Side of Change Leadership," 39–43.

will be impacted. Although the situation may warrant cuts to personnel, a leader must work hard to ensure that those receiving the "pink slips" are handled with kindness and empathy. Leaders do well to remember that humans are not assets or widgets; they have feelings, emotions, responsibilities, and ambitions. When facing the prospect of losing a job, they will face an enormous amount of stress. Therefore, any organizational decision which will cause someone hardship should be prayed over, and other options should be considered before it is acted upon. Godly leaders will sacrifice their own personal achievements to help those under their leadership to prosper to the best of their abilities.

Leaders do not have a choice as to whether they will deal with change; it is inevitable. Therefore, leaders must be equipped with skills to successfully manage organizational change. Paton provides the following:

- Communication skills are essential and must be applied both within and outside the managing team, maintaining motivation and providing leadership to all concerned.
- The ability to facilitate and orchestrate group and individual activities is crucial.
- Negotiation and influencing skills are invaluable.
- It is essential that both planning and control procedures are employed.
- The ability to manage on all planes, upward, downward and within the peer group, must be acquired.
- Knowledge of, and the facility to influence the rationale for change is essential.[8]

This brief list shows that a leader who is managing change must be adaptive, multi-faceted, flexible, knowledgeable, optimistic, and a great communicator. Organizational change creates a ripple effect throughout an organization, which means a process change in the manufacturing department may impact research and development or human resources departments. Organizations are living systems which are always in a state of flux, so when one part moves, the others move also. According to Tim Creasey, Director of Research and Development for Prosci, change management can be defined as "the process, tools, and techniques to manage the people side of change

---

8. Paton and McCalman, *Change Management*, 17.

to achieve a required business outcome."[9] When we introduce change to a client organization, we know we are ultimately going to be impacting two or more of the following four parts of the organization:

1. Processes
2. Systems
3. Organization structure
4. Job roles[10]

Each of these four sections directly impacts the people or the "people-side" of the organization, which makes all organizational change impactive on the workforce. Thus, a better way to exhibit this structure might be,

1. Processes and people who run them
2. Systems and those who operate them
3. Organization structure of the workforce
4. Personnel job roles

Although this change may seem superficial, it keeps the effect on each member of the organization at the forefront in the change management process.

Although "change management" is the accepted phrase in management theory, a better moniker might be "leadership management," as it places the onus upon leaders to oversee change with the end goal of blessing the workforce and improving the organization. Leaders and managers are two very different types of people. A manager may be able to establish a process by which change is accomplished, while a leader will embrace change and create something from it to grow the organization. Kotter provides a useful side-by-side comparison chart clarifying the distinctions between leadership and management.[11]

---

9. Voehl and Harrington, *Change Management*, 5.
10. Ibid.
11. Kotter, *A Force for Change*, 139.

Leadership Produces change and movement	Management Produces order and consistency
1. Establishes direction • Creates a vision • Clarifies the big picture • Sets strategies	1. Planning and budgeting • Establishes agendas • Sets timetables • Allocates resources
2. Aligns people • Communicates goals • Seeks commitment • Builds teams, coalitions and alliances	2. Organizing and staffing • Provides structure • Makes job placements • Establishes rules and procedures
3. Motivates and inspires • Energizes • Empowers subordinates & colleagues • Satisfies unmet needs	3. Controlling and problem solving • Develops incentives • Generates creative solutions • Takes corrective action

Figure 2

Leaders are often described as those who "establish," "align," "motivate," and "inspire," while task managers are those who "plan," "budget," "organize," and "control." Each of the leadership attributes are forward-thinking and do not rely on past practices. The leader wants change to benefit the entire organization and sees himself as a conduit or cheerleader in attaining goals and fulfilling visions. The leader is also very aware that change is a team effort, and many leaders and followers must be involved in the process from start to finish. According to McCalman,

> The idea that wholesale change can be led and directly influenced by one change leader is a fallacy. What is required is an organizational network of leaders all working together on the change initiative. We would reject the transformational leader in the singular in favour of a network of change leaders who advance the cultural changes as advocated by the overarching change leader. There has to be a symbolic leader, who walks the walk as well as talking the talk, but they cannot achieve cultural change at the transformational level by themselves; they need a support team. This also fits with what Hutton (1994) classifies as a "cast of characters."[12]

This "cast of characters" actively participating in and having ownership for the change process can make the change both palatable and beneficial.

---

12. McCalman, *Leading Cultural Change*, 6.

Creating a culture of change is the best model for dealing with planned and unforeseen organizational change. Although the overarching cultural construct of postmodernism and its basis in fluidity and ambiguity may make the change process more difficult, understanding the mindset of postmodernists will help in finding areas of agreement upon which to build. Paulien provides an optimistic approach for Christian leaders to embrace by authentically reaching the hearts and minds of postmodernists:

> Living in an age in which image is king, postmodern individuals place a high premium on humility, honesty, and authenticity in interpersonal relationships. They feel it is better to be honest about one's weaknesses and handicaps than to craft an image or "play the audience." Postmoderns not only have a strong sense of brokenness; they are willing to share that brokenness honestly with friends they consider safe. Humility and authenticity are, of course, very central attributes of genuine Christian faith. Genuine confession is nothing less than telling the truth about yourself. In secular modernism humility was not prized. It was thought to be demeaning to human value. When modernism was at its height, people needed to be humble only if they had plenty to be humble about! Postmodernism, on the other hand, places a high value on genuineness. This suggests to me that God is bringing the culture to the place where it values one of the greatest testing truths of the Christian tradition. This is a golden opportunity for genuine Christian faith.[13]

Hence, the Christian leader living out his faith with authenticity and transparency will be able to build a relationship of trust with the postmodernist and be able to harness that relationship to work toward common goals in a change environment. Moving an entire organization into a culture which seeks, embraces, and enjoys change is not an easy task, but it will successfully prepare the entity to handle even the greatest challenges with an eye toward triumph. Hackman and Johnson provide four change behaviors necessary for an organization to embrace and capitalize on change:

- External Monitoring—scanning the environment to identify threats and opportunities from customers, clients, suppliers, government policies, market trends, and so on. Includes reading industry reports, attending professional meetings, talking to customers, studying competitors, and conducting market research. Monitoring also

---

13. Paulien, *Everlasting Gospel*, 58.

incorporates analyzing the information and interpreting events to lay the foundation for change.

- Envisioning Change—creating an inspiring vision to encourage followers to commit to change; connecting with the values, goals, and ideals of followers.
- Encouraging Innovative Thinking—sparking innovative thinking in others and in oneself; proposing innovative ideas.
- Taking Personal Risks—stepping out to push for change in the face of opposition, which may result in loss of job, reputation, or career.[14]

In aligning with the aforementioned leadership attributes, each of these behaviors also has an eye toward the future, seeking ways to anticipate changes which may be helpful to the organization. Again, each of these requires a team approach with every member monitoring, envisioning, encouraging, and taking risks. Although these are required for the leader, each member should also be encouraged to emulate these behaviors.

Berstene sounds the alarm for a collaborative approach to change by motivating everyone to be part of the solution rather than be part of the problem:

> Change management is an all-hands, participative activity. It is not a dictate that comes down from on high and then presto, all of a sudden, we are working in the new way—although there are some bosses who think it works like this. We all could identify one or two of these misguided creatures. Instead, change management requires all of us to participate actively. We may be team members designing the new way of working or part of the team creating the procedures and training to help everyone understand how the new system will work. Perhaps like many, we are on the receiving end of the change edict. No matter how we are affected, we need to participate actively—those of us rebels who are trying to resist the new and keep things as they were. After all, the old process was working, and we don't want to mess with something that works.[15]

When an employee has a voice in the change process, he will know that his input is appreciated. Also, his contribution plays the important role of helping to ensure that his particular office or division is considered favorably when final decisions are made.

14. Hackman and Johnson, *Leadership*, 52.
15. Berstene, "Resiliency," 39–40.

The Leadership Imperative

Those who choose to act out in anger and refrain from engaging in the change process are removing both themselves and those they may represent from the brainstorming or negotiating process, thus reducing their chance for a favorable outcome. This is how our system of governance works in the United States. Each state has several representatives to argue on behalf of the desires of the constituents. If the elected official is not present, the voice of the people will not be heard, and their issues will not be considered. In a micro-organizational setting, this is also the case, as each department should have and use every opportunity to present its case. Berstene continues,

> The best stories of change management success come from those case studies where management planted the seed, provided the environment for the seed to take root, and then allowed the change to grow through active participation of the employees. These leaders participate enough to keep the process moving and to provide guidance as needed, but they do not get in the way.[16]

Leaders provide the initial vision for change, invite a large swath of participants representing all facets of the organization, then set them free to work toward a successful outcome. Although oversight during the beginning of the change initiative is likely, when the group takes hold of the vision, the leader can assess from afar and provide support as necessary. The horizontal approach to change management creates the prospect of a "win-win" scenario where everyone throughout the organization is a respected participant while aligning with the leader's vision.

The most problematic form of unplanned change is a catastrophe or crisis which jolts the organization and triggers instant fear. America has witnessed its share of calamitous events over the past twenty years, with the terrorist attacks of 9/11 being the most prolific. Each time the United States deals with crises by terrorists, hurricanes, or other unforeseen disasters, the citizens look to their leader, the president, for direction and assurance. After the attacks of 9/11, President George W. Bush spoke with a megaphone to the firefighters at Ground Zero, both to encourage them and to promise them that the perpetrators would face justice. The President's words gave the crowd, and those listening throughout America, assurance that their leader was on top of the situation and was working on their behalf for justice to be accomplished. In times of crises, leaders take the spotlight and have the responsibility to calm fears, remedy the situation,

16. Ibid.

and show courage. When managed wisely, fears can be relieved and people can refocus on their mission. Conversely, if a leader uses the opportunity for self-aggrandizement, the leader will be minimized, and an opposition leader will likely arise. In a crisis, Christian leaders have the opportunity to emulate Christ by displaying courage, grace, honor, and accountability. If the Christian leader succumbs to fear and despair, those following may do likewise. Standing firm with patience and endurance while providing wise counsel during a catastrophe can make the difference between life and death, or fear and calm. The Scriptures are replete with counsel for those facing turmoil and the temptation to fear:

- So do not fear, for I am with you; do not be dismayed, for I am your God. I will strengthen you and help you; I will uphold you with my righteous right hand.[17]
- When I am afraid, I put my trust in you.[18]
- Do not be anxious about anything, but in every situation, by prayer and petition, with thanksgiving, present your requests to God. And the peace of God, which transcends all understanding, will guard your hearts and your minds in Christ Jesus.[19]
- Peace I leave with you; my peace I give you. I do not give to you as the world gives. Do not let your hearts be troubled and do not be afraid.[20]
- For the Spirit God gave us does not make us timid, but gives us power, love and self-discipline.[21]
- But now, this is what the Lord says . . . Fear not, for I have redeemed you; I have summoned you by name; you are mine.[22]
- Anxiety weighs down the heart, but a kind word cheers it up.[23]
- Even though I walk through the darkest valley, I will fear no evil, for you are with me; your rod and your staff, they comfort me.[24]

17. Isa 41:10 (NIV).
18. Ps 56:3 (NIV).
19. Phil 4:6–7 (NIV).
20. John 14:27 (NIV).
21. 2 Tim 1:7 (NIV).
22. Isa 43:1 (NIV).
23. Prov 12:25 (NIV).
24. Ps 23:4 (NIV).

- Have I not commanded you? Be strong and courageous. Do not be afraid; do not be discouraged, for the LORD your God will be with you wherever you go.[25]

- Therefore do not worry about tomorrow, for tomorrow will worry about itself. Each day has enough trouble of its own.[26]

- Humble yourselves, therefore, under God's mighty hand, that he may lift you up in due time.[27]

The Bible presents the topic of fear on many occasions throughout the Old and New Testament. Life is filled with sudden calamities, and God uses them to draw his people closer to himself. Scripture provides a host of wonderful examples of leaders who courageously followed God during trials, thus providing hope to those who followed. Examples of these leaders include Noah, Moses, Joshua, David, Daniel, Nehemiah, John, Peter, Paul, and many more. Each of these leaders faced extraordinary circumstances which propelled them to rely on God during a disaster.

In the postmodern era, fear, doubt, and worry are ubiquitous as more and more people abandon God and rely solely on themselves or other fallible persons for support. Many colleges have created "safe spaces" for students to congregate in a place where no one may hurt their feelings. Young men are raised to run and hide during a crisis, instead of courageously fending off a potential attacker and protecting others around them. Postmodernity has become a period of cowardice, as fewer persons are willing to lead and protect others because they are often consumed with their own self-interests. Historically, competition yielded a winner and a loser, but in postmodernity, everyone wins, regardless of effort or achievement. This era is in dire need of leaders who hold fast to something well beyond themselves and are willing to sacrifice for others. Fullan writes,

> Clearly these are exciting times—there is a lot going on. Not the least of these developments is the new realization that leadership is key to large-scale improvement yet must be radically different than it has been. Further, effective leadership is in very short supply. We can therefore expect to see leadership development initiatives dominating the scene over the next decade. Leadership required in a culture of change, however, is not straightforward.

25. Josh 1:9.
26. Matt 6:34 (NIV).
27. 1 Pet 5:6–7.

Leading Change in a Culture of Fluidity

We are living in chaotic conditions. Thus leaders must be able to operate under complex, uncertain circumstances.[28]

Although crises may create ambiguity and chaos, the leader must react in a way that shows resolve, courage, and consistency.

Organizational leaders who understand that crises may come at any time will be the best equipped to handle them. Although it is almost impossible to predict crises, leaders can be prepared to lead during calamity. As defined by Pearson and Clair, an organizational crisis is "a low probability, high impact situation that is perceived by critical stakeholders to threaten the viability of the organization and is characterized by ambiguity of cause, effect, and means of resolution."[29] Although it would be challenging to list every conceivable calamity, Hackman provides ten types of crises which cover most scenarios:

1. Public perception: negative stories about the organization's products, personnel, or services; negative rumors; blogs and websites
2. Natural disasters: tornadoes, hurricanes, mudslides, wildfires, blizzards, earthquakes, volcanic eruptions
3. Product or service: product recalls, food-borne illnesses, concern about products and services generated by the media
4. Terrorist attacks: bombings, hijackings, abductions, poisonings
5. Economic: cash shortages, bankruptcies, hostile takeovers, accounting scandals
6. Human resource: workplace violence, strikes, labor unrest, discrimination, sexual harassment, school and workplace shootings, theft, fraud
7. Industrial: mine collapses, nuclear accidents, fires, explosions
8. Oil and chemical spills: tanker and railway spills, pipeline and well leaks
9. Transportation: train derailments, plane crashes, truck accidents, multi-vehicle pileups
10. Outside environment: collapse of financial systems, rising fuel prices, deregulation, nationalization of private companies, mortgage crisis[30]

---

28. Fullan, *Culture of Change*, xii.
29. Pearson and Clair, *Academy of Management Review*, 59–76.
30. Hackman and Johnson, *Leadership*, 411.

This list is daunting to organizational leaders, as most of these situations create significant challenges regarding logistics and finances. However, leaders who are adept in crisis management will deal first with the immediate issues surrounding the event, resulting in an open flow of honest communication to those impacted. While the truth can be very painful, especially at the onset of a crisis, people will ultimately handle the truth from a sincere leader much better than deception which is intended to relay panic. Leaders have a responsibility to communicate early and often during a crisis, while showing empathy and steadiness. Bruce Condit, the Vice President of Allegiance Capital provides seven critical steps to manage a crisis:

1. *Have a plan*—Every plan begins with clear objectives. The objectives during any crisis are to protect any individual (employee or public) who may be endangered by the crisis, ensure the key audiences are kept informed, and the organization survives. This written plan should include specific actions that will be taken in the event of a crisis.

2. *Identify a spokesperson*—If the crisis could potentially impact the health or well-being of customers, the general public or employees, it may attract media attention. To ensure your company speaks with one voice and delivers a clear consistent message, a spokesperson must be identified as well as prepared to answer media questions and participate in interviews.

3. *Be honest and open*—Nothing generates more negative media coverage than a lack of honesty and transparency. Therefore, being as open and transparent as possible can help stop rumors and defuse a potential media frenzy. This transparency must be projected through all communications channels: news interviews, social media, internal announcements, etc.

4. *Keep employees informed*—Maintaining an informed workforce helps ensure that business continues to flow as smoothly as possible. It also minimizes the internal rumor mill that may lead to employees posting false reports on social media.

5. *Communicate with customers and suppliers*—You do not want customers and suppliers to learn about your crisis through the media. Information on any crisis pertaining to your organization should come from you first. Part of the crisis communications plan must

include customers and suppliers and how they will be regularly updated during the event.

6. *Update early and often*—It is better to over-communicate than to allow rumors to fill the void. Issue summary statements, updated action plans, and new developments as early and as often as possible. Remember that with today's social media and cable news outlets, we live in a time of the 24/7 news cycle. Your crisis plan must do the same.

7. *Don't forget social media*—The Ebola crisis and other recent major news events have all confirmed that social media is one of the most important channels of communications. Be sure to establish a social media team to monitor, post, and react to social media activity throughout the crisis.[31]

All change, whether planned, unplanned, or even catastrophic, requires bold, patient, and courageous leaders to set the tone, allay fears, present confidence and competence, and communicate an optimistic path forward. Christian leaders have a wealth of examples, imperatives, and narratives throughout the entire canon of Scripture to consider and apply. Although the crisis situations for the leaders in Scripture were unique, the principles of leadership have not changed. During times of change, leaders have an optimal opportunity to lead by faith under some of the harshest conditions, while relying fully on Christ for the process and the outcome.

---

31. Condit, "7 Critical Steps."

8

Four C's of Christocentric Leadership
Courage, Credibility, Character, and Compassion

> *Furthermore, you shall select out of all the people able men who fear God, men of truth, those who hate dishonest gain; and you shall place these over them as leaders of thousands, of hundreds, of fifties and of tens.*
>
> —EXODUS 18:21 (NASB)

MOST BOOKS WRITTEN ON the topic of leadership list attributes of a successful leader. These characteristics are admirable and worthy of pursuit. For Christian leaders, the goal is to align oneself with the traits of Jesus Christ, emulating him and seeking his will. Four qualities seem to encapsulate the essence of what defines a Christian leader: courage, credibility, character, and compassion. The Exodus verse above harkens back to Moses trying to lead the Israelites and singlehandedly make decisions for them. As leaders are often tempted to do, Moses micromanaged the affairs of his people and did not entrust even the small tasks to others to accomplish. Noticing that Moses was overwhelmed, his father-in-law Jethro intervened and counseled Moses to appoint other men to handle the lesser matters while judging the serious matters himself. Jethro did not recommend picking just anyone to lead, however; he counseled Moses to appoint God-fearing, honest men

Four C's of Christocentric Leadership

to ensure that decisions were just, fair, and honorable. This same counsel should be considered today when leadership positions are to be filled or when future leaders are mentored.

Leaders who are courageous (not timid), credible (not hypocritical), of sound character (not prone to folly), and compassionate (not hardhearted) are able to lead wisely, even through the chaos and ambiguity of the postmodern age. These traits, however, are not sufficient, for they must be rooted in something (or someone) deeper for them to be effective. Albert Mohler calls this "convictional leadership" and explains it this way:

> When a leader walks into a room, a passion for truth had better enter with him. Authentic leadership does not emerge out of a vacuum. The leadership that matters most is convictional—deeply convictional. This quality of leadership springs from those foundational beliefs about everything else. Convictions are not merely beliefs we hold; they are those beliefs that hold us in their grip. We would not know who we are but for these bedrock beliefs, and without them we would not know how to lead.[1]

Mohler rightly points out that leadership must have a foundation for it to be efficacious. For the Christian leader, the foundation is Christ and his word, as illustrated by the Apostle Paul to the Church in Corinth:

> According to the grace of God given to me, like a skilled master builder I laid a foundation, and someone else is building upon it. Let each one take care how he builds upon it. For no one can lay a foundation other than that which is laid, which is Jesus Christ. Now if anyone builds on the foundation with gold, silver, precious stones, wood, hay, straw— each one's work will become manifest, for the Day will disclose it, because it will be revealed by fire, and the fire will test what sort of work each one has done. If the work that anyone has built on the foundation survives, he will receive a reward. If anyone's work is burned up, he will suffer loss, though he himself will be saved, but only as through fire.[2]

Even the greatest leadership attributes will not stand the test of time if they are not grounded in the one who created and perfectly exemplifies these traits: the Lord Jesus Christ. Secular leaders may also show courage, credibility, character, and compassion. However, when leaders lack the power of the Holy Spirit, they limit their impact. Rather than leading *Soli Deo Gloria*,

---

1. Mohler, *Conviction to Lead*, 21.
2. 1 Cor 3:10–15.

they venerate themselves. Furthermore, as warned by Paul, all works which are not built upon the foundation of Christ are worthy only to be disposed of as kindling (1 Cor 3:15). Christian leadership requires a constant effort to ensure all actions are rooted in and completed for the glory of God alone.

Courage

One of the most significant tasks of a leader is that of making decisions. Organizational leaders must continually assess employee requests, disagreements, budgets, personnel changes, and proposals, and make fair and impartial decisions to the benefits of both the organization and the members. These decisions often come at a significant cost (either emotional or monetary), and will often benefit one party over another. Consequently, leaders must exercise wisdom and courage in decision-making to ensure that the "right" or "best" decision is made. Often, it is easier to make decisions which will cause the least amount of disorder, even though the decision may be wrong or ill-conceived. For example, an employee presents a complaint against a supervisor for discrimination and threatens legal action if he is not promoted. After investigating the situation, the evidence reveals no discrimination had occurred. Understanding that a lawsuit may be costly and create a public image issue, it may be tempting to provide the promotion or some payment to alleviate the situation. In doing so, the immediate problem may go away, but the leader is tacitly approving of a deception scheme on the part of the employee. The right decision is to inform the employee that the case was investigated and that no evidence was found to support the claim of discrimination. Courage is required to make the right decision, regardless of the potentially negative consequence. In making decisions, leaders are both setting precedence for future situations and showing everyone where they stand.

Leaders willing to do what is right in the face of considerable opposition are in the minority, for many simply appease others just to get along. Courage is linked to every other virtue, as it provides the impetus to create the most honorable outcome. Heft notes,

> Is it possible for a person to possess any virtue if he or she does not also possess the virtue of courage? Think of any virtue and ask yourself if it can really be a virtue if the person who has it lacks courage. If a person thinks she is generous, but lacks courage, does not that mean that she will give only when it does not hurt, when it does not

Four C's of Christocentric Leadership

cost her much personally? If a person thinks he is compassionate, but expresses compassion only when such an act would be well seen by others, does that person really possess the virtue of compassion? If people pride themselves on their honesty but do not speak out when it results in disapproval by influential persons and leads to a loss of their livelihood, can they in fact be thought to have the virtue of honesty? If then courage is the guarantee of all other virtues, why is not cowardice one of the seven capital sins?[3]

As the postmodern era struggles with objective truth, it is hard for leaders of the prevailing mindset to act courageously in protecting anything worthwhile, for the value of any cause can change at any moment. Proponents of absolute truth understand and appreciate the value of defending something, as it is inherently a battle of right versus wrong. For Christian leaders, honesty, fairness, and justice are worth the fight, as once they are lost, there is little left of redemptive value. This is the reason Christians will fight so courageously for the unborn; they understand that this battle is lost when the culture has decided human life is of little value. Once a culture determines that human beings lack worth, people will act on their worst impulses and hedonistic tendencies in their treatment of others. Toward the end of the 2016 Vice Presidential Debate, Indiana Governor Mike Pence was provided time for closing comments. Instead of making a populace appeal on issues where most Americans agree, he chose instead to make a strong case against abortion, in favor of unborn babies. This decision showed courage, as it would likely offend those in the anti-life movement. However, leading with conviction includes using every opportunity to take a stand for truth and to make a case for biblical values, regardless of the consequences.

The biblical Daniel narrative also provides a powerful example of courage under fire. Daniel was a faithful servant of King Darius and earned his favor by living, working, and speaking righteously. His reputation was faultless, as he consistently and quietly worked hard and served others with dignity. The source of Daniel's right living was God, to whom he prayed and who he worshiped each day. As others (presidents and satraps) observed Daniel's life, they became jealous and indignant while plotting a deceptive action against him. To trap Daniel, they convinced King Darius to sign an injunction against anyone worshiping a person or deity other than the King. Daniel, fully understanding the consequences of praying to God, continued

---

3. Heft, "The Courage to Lead," 294.

his worship without pause. As a result, Daniel was thrown into a den of lions as a method of execution. Daniel prayed to God for deliverance and was heard. This narrative is an exceptional example for Christian leaders facing tough decisions. Although leaders are not guaranteed that they will be spared from the outcomes of making brave decisions, they can rest assured that they have both honored God and maintained a clear conscience. The Scriptures are replete with examples of courageous leaders who were willing to sacrifice everything in their stand for objective truth and its God. Moses led the Israelites out of bondage in Egypt; Noah constructed a ship in preparation for a massive flood, while likely being mocked and ridiculed; Joshua bravely led the Israelites into the promised land; Nehemiah, against all odds, reconstructed the temple; and nearly all of the Apostles were martyred for spreading the gospel of Jesus Christ. When God calls one of his followers to lead, he equips them and sends them out into some of the harshest conditions to courageously fight for and defend truth. Michael writes,

> The great challenge for many Christian leaders today is standing strong for the cause of righteousness. In an age of conciliation and compliance, many persons in leadership positions find it difficult to stay above the fray of wavering convictions. The secular pressures of political correctness, the insatiable desires for success, the fretful concern over job security, and the lack of principled confidence in one's beliefs all contribute to a pattern of weak leadership. Researcher George Barna writes, "Surprisingly few people have the internal strength to stand up for what is right. We call this courage. God's leaders are always people of great courage."[4]

Courage is one of the defining marks of Christian leaders as they live out their faith in the midst of an increasingly godless generation.

Christological courage can only derive its strength from God himself, as man is by nature feeble and easily disheartened. Courage in the face of adversity must be managed by prayer, the only source of communion that humanity has with the Father. The word of God is his primary communication to his people, and the proper response to it is adoration, confession, thanksgiving, and supplication. These four aspects of prayer encompass requests, repentance, and praise to God, which he lays out as an example in the Lord's Prayer (Matt 6:9–13). Based on his forgiveness, Christians can boldly approach the throne of grace with requests, such as the need for

---

4. Michael, *Spurgeon on Leadership*, 138.

courage in each predicament. Christ uses the humble to do his work, even leading through some of the worst trials in life with strength and confidence. In the Petrine pericope, the Apostle exhorts the Christian leaders to "Humble yourselves, therefore, under the mighty hand of God so that at the proper time he may exalt you, casting all your anxieties on him, because he cares for you."[5] While the world's mode of leadership revolves around prideful persons, God's methodology has always elevated the humble to perform great works. The humble are those with the utmost strength. According to MacArthur,

> Spiritual strength for believers is essentially an attitude of courage, and it includes such virtues as the courage of convictions, courage to be uncompromising, courage to confront error and false doctrine, and courage to face intimidation and persecution and remain faithful to what is right. A strong Christian is one who lives by principle rather than the whim of opinion.[6]

Unlike the winds of postmodernism, which move leaders from one principle to the next, Christian leaders may stand firm in the unchangeable truth with courage and conviction.

Credibility

Before the Civil War, Major Thomas "Stonewall" Jackson was a Philosophy professor at the Virginia Military Institute (VMI), and he was considered to be "VMI's worst teacher."[7] In the classroom, Jackson was disrespected, mocked, and maligned, not because of his lack of intellect, but because he was unable to translate his knowledge to his students in a meaningful fashion. He wrote out his lectures, read them verbatim, and chose not to elaborate, answer questions, or clarify matters when students did not understand.[8] Several unsuccessful attempts were made to remove him from the classroom. One of the greatest generals in history had zero credibility with his students or colleagues. Shortly thereafter, the Civil War began, and Major Jackson became one of the most feared and respected officers in military history. If the Civil War had never begun, Thomas Jackson would not

---

5. 1 Pet 5:6–7.
6. MacArthur, *The Pillars of Christian Character*, 121.
7. Gwynne, *Rebel*, 15.
8. Ibid., 15.

even be a footnote in American history. Everything changed for Jackson in 1861 when he was commissioned by General Robert E. Lee to muster his new command in Harpers Ferry and prepare for war with the Union Army. Although Jackson lacked credibility in the classroom, he gained the respect of his troops, his superior officers, and his enemies as a battlefield commander. Jackson was steadfast and uncompromising, an idealist who was the "go-to" guy in battle. He was trusted to do what was right for his people regardless of the opposition. General Jackson was a God-fearing man who trusted in the words of Scripture. With a strong belief in the sovereignty of God and his providential will over all matters, Jackson did not fear death, knowing that his life was in God's hands. In Jackson's personal journal, he penned a discussion that he had with Captain John D. Imboden:

> "Captain, my religious belief teaches me to feel as safe in battle as in bed. God has fixed the time for my death. I do not concern myself about that, but to be always ready, no matter when it may overtake me." He added, after a pause, looking me full in the face: "That is the way all men should live, and then all would be equally brave."[9]

Jackson's credibility grew over time through repeated battlefield successes and by his desire to fearlessly pursue the causes he believed in.

Dwight D. Eisenhower once said, "A platoon leader doesn't get his platoon to go by getting up and shouting and saying, 'I am smarter. I am bigger. I am stronger. I am the leader.' He gets men to go along with him because they want to do it for him and they believe in him."[10] In its most basic form, leadership requires followers. One may have researched the greatest leadership techniques and followed a myriad of gurus to understand best the attributes needed to lead, but if he looks behind him to see an empty space, he is not a leader. Positions and rank do not equal leadership. Optimally, they provide someone with an opportunity to combine positional authority with genuine leadership. A leader is someone whom others deem credible, capable, trustworthy, and competent, and believe in enough to follow. Credibility is not a trait which can be quickly garnered; it must be earned over time through experience, trials, training, and education. Also, it must also be coupled with the significant characteristic of courage as discussed. Credibility allows leaders to connect with others, to influence them and guide them with confidence.

---

9. Selby, *Stonewall Jackson*, 25.
10. Hughes and Beatty, *Becoming a Strategic Leader*, 162.

Four C's of Christocentric Leadership

Leadership credibility is vital to organizational success. Because credibility and influence are connected, a leader will be unable to achieve goals and inspire others to do their best if he is not respected. According to Hughes,

> Influencing others strategically is virtually impossible if you don't have credibility. Credibility involves two broad dimensions: expertise and character. By expertise, we mean technical competence as well as organizational and industry knowledge, and the latter two are particularly important when thinking about strategic leadership. Building organizational and industry knowledge requires looking beyond one's specific job boundaries and responsibilities and taking an enterprise-wide perspective. Without willingness and ability to do so, one's chance of influencing others strategically are significantly diminished.[11]

Credibility is one of twenty-two leadership characteristics measured by the Campbell Leadership Index (CLI). Credibility on the CLI is measured by the following descriptions,

- *Candid:* Open and honest when dealing with others.
- *Credible:* Worthy of trust, believable.
- *Deceptive:* Conceals the truth for selfish reasons.
- *Ethical:* Lives within society's standards of right and wrong.
- *Scheming:* Develops sly and devious plans.
- *Trustworthy:* Inspires trust and confidence.[12]

The CLI's use of both positive and negative characteristics is helpful for leaders in discovering strengths and weaknesses regarding credibility with the goal of improvement toward more effective leadership. It appears that all discussions regarding credibility eventually lead to the importance of character. Although character is the next trait to be considered, a helpful segue to this topic is provided by Albert Mohler:

> No leader can be effective without character, but character does not ensure that a leader is effective. There are many people with sterling character who are not leaders. A good leader stands out when character is matched to competence and the central virtue of knowing what to do. Most of us think of credibility in moral terms,

---

11. Ibid., 136.
12. Campbell, "Good Leaders Are Credible Leaders," 29.

and with good reason. Credibility defines our ability to trust, and that trust is a matter of character. However, leadership requires trust in something beyond who the leader is. True credibility rests in the ability of others to trust what the leader can do.[13]

As in the case of Stonewall Jackson, credibility arises when moral character and competence meet, inspiring trust from others.

Character

If a random group of people was asked to make a list of leaders whom they admire the most and then ask them why they chose those people, there is a strong likelihood that "character" would be at the top of the list. People tend to respect and follow those with a strong moral character, one who holds fast to a set of beliefs and is willing to fight for them. Character is often associated with one's reputation. The character of a person involves visceral values, while the reputation is the outward perceptions of others based on whether the words, actions, and beliefs are in alignment. If a member of a community is said to be respected, valued, and honored, it can be assumed that his moral character is strong. Like all other terms in postmodernity, character must be clearly defined to ensure each person does not assess objective values based solely on personal opinions. For this, the Scriptures can be consulted, as the Apostle Paul provides a list of required character traits for church leaders. Although this list is mandated for pastors, elders, and bishops, it also provides strong attributes for every leader to aspire toward. Paul writes,

> Here is a trustworthy saying: Whoever aspires to be an overseer desires a noble task. Now the overseer is to be above reproach, faithful to his wife, temperate, self-controlled, respectable, hospitable, able to teach, not given to drunkenness, not violent but gentle, not quarrelsome, not a lover of money. He must manage his own family well and see that his children obey him, and he must do so in a manner worthy of full respect. (If anyone does not know how to manage his own family, how can he take care of God's church?) He must not be a recent convert, or he may become conceited and fall under the same judgment as the devil. He

---

13. Mohler, *Conviction to Lead*, 83.

must also have a good reputation with outsiders so that he will not fall into disgrace and into the devil's trap.[14]

Therefore, the contemporary Christian leader should be honest, faithful to family, patient, cool and collected, honorable, skilled in teaching and training others, giving (not greedy), sober-minded, gentle, and have a good reputation among others. If a Christian leader examines himself against these attributes, he will be able to best assess his current moral character. Paul sought the strongest leaders to oversee the people of God, to ensure that they were not misled and that they were examples of godliness. These successful leaders will provide solid biblical instruction, care for those with needs, and lead others to a closer walk with Christ. All Christian leaders should take up this mantle of leadership within their places of work, communities, and in their homes.

General Norman Schwarzkopf points to the significance of character: "Leadership is a potent combination of strategy and character. But if you must be without one, be without strategy."[15] General Schwarzkopf's pithy assessment of the importance of character is worthy to be considered. When hiring officials conduct interviews for positions at various levels of organizations, the primary focus is competence. Organizations want the most capable people to write code, practice law, engineer products, perform surgery, or fix a vehicle. Unfortunately, character receives little consideration in the hiring process and often creates some unintended consequences. The skilled code writer is addicted to illegal drugs and uses his skills to hack the corporate pay system to steal funds; the powerful attorney demands sexual favors for payment from indigent clients; the genius engineer utilizes work assets to design systems to start his own business; the top-rated surgeon works on patients after long nights of heavy drinking; and the mechanic convinces his customers to call him on his personal phone to perform jobs "off the books." The most competent and skilled workers void of a strong moral framework can wreak havoc on any organization. Anthony Harrigan, president of the United States Business and Industrial Council asserts the following:

> The role of character has been the key factor in the rise and fall of nations. And one can be sure that America is no exception to this rule of history. We won't survive as a country because we are smarter or more sophisticated but because we are—we hope—stronger

14. 1 Tim 3:1–7 (NIV).
15. Maxwell, *21 Irrefutable Laws*, 64.

> inwardly. In short, character is the only effective bulwark against internal and external forces that lead to a country's disintegration or collapse.[16]

Harrigan's warning must be heeded before America reaches such a point of collapse; many would argue that we are not far from that destination.

At the time of this writing, the 2016 Presidential race has concluded and America has chosen its new leader. On January 20th, President Donald Trump placed his hand on a Bible and swore to protect and defend the Constitution of the United States. Unfortunately, America has arrived at a time when character is not the most important trait to consider in electing the leader of the free world. Both major parties' candidates were continually accused of gross hyperbole, lies, perversion (sexual innuendo, harassment, and even assault), the theft and transfer of government secrets, pay-to-play schemes, arrogance, and tax evasion. As in the historical incident regarding President Bill Clinton and Monica Lewinsky, America looked the other way. Truth, honor, courage, character, credibility, and compassion seem to be a thing of the past, of a bygone era. Thankfully, the Scriptures provide numerous examples of godless kings who had destroyed the morality of nations being replaced by God-fearing leaders. America is in desperate need of leaders with strong character who are seeking the heart and will of God. Faithful Christian leaders will multiply to create new leaders after them, and hopefully a stronger generation of future leaders will make major changes to the moral fiber of this nation and throughout the world. Reeder writes,

> Genuine Christian leadership must be learned from God's Word, developed through disciple making, nurtured in God's church, and then transported to the world. When this happens, we can anticipate a consistent reproduction of multiplication leaders who have been transformed by biblical leadership. It is God's chain reaction. A transformed leader produces more transformed leaders—leaders who have been mentored within the church, then sent out to impact the world.[17]

Reeder's assertion that the church is the training ground for leadership is poignant. Just as soldiers spend months in boot camp preparing for the real battle, Christian leaders must prepare themselves spiritually before leading others.

---

16. Ibid., 64.
17. Reeder and Gragg, *The Leadership Dynamic*, 11.

Four C's of Christocentric Leadership

Compassion

Although acts of kindness rarely receive much media attention, each day, people throughout the world are meeting the needs of others through compassion and mercy. *Baker's Dictionary* defines compassion as:

> That (human) disposition which fuels acts of kindness and mercy. Compassion, a form of love, is aroused within us when we are confronted with those who suffer or are vulnerable. Compassion often produces action to alleviate the suffering, but sometimes geographical distances or lack of means prevent people from acting upon their compassionate feelings.[18]

Compassion derives from the Greek term *splagchnizomai*, meaning to be moved in the inward parts[19] and relays the idea of compassion as a visceral, internal, or "gut" reaction to seeing or hearing of someone in need or suffering. Compassion as an intrinsic quality is only beneficial if an outward act of mercy follows. Christ exhorted his disciples to follow compassion with acts of mercy:

> By this we know love, that he laid down his life for us, and we ought to lay down our lives for the brothers. But if anyone has the world's goods and sees his brother in need, yet closes his heart against him, how does God's love abide in him? Little children, let us not love in word or talk but in deed and in truth.[20]

Christ is encouraging his followers to not simply feel bad for someone in need, but to then follow the feeling by meeting that need.

In the familiar narrative regarding the parable of the Good Samaritan, Christ is answering a lawyer's questions regarding how to attain eternal life by asking what the law reads. The lawyer quickly responds by quoting Levitical law about loving God and one's neighbor. The lawyer, believing he was fulfilling this law, inquired further about who should be considered one's neighbor. The answer to this question probably shocked the lawyer, as he likely believed he only needed to serve his fellow Jew. Christ responds,

> A man was going down from Jerusalem to Jericho, and he fell among robbers, who stripped him and beat him and departed, leaving him half dead. Now by chance a priest was going down

---

18. Elwell, "Compassion," para. 1.
19. Strong, *Exhaustive Concordance*, 333.
20. 1 John 3:16–18.

that road, and when he saw him he passed by on the other side. So likewise a Levite, when he came to the place and saw him, passed by on the other side. But a Samaritan, as he journeyed, came to where he was, and when he saw him, he had compassion. He went to him and bound up his wounds, pouring on oil and wine. Then he set him on his own animal and brought him to an inn and took care of him. And the next day he took out two denarii and gave them to the innkeeper, saying, "Take care of him, and whatever more you spend, I will repay you when I come back." Which of these three, do you think, proved to be a neighbor to the man who fell among the robbers? He said, "The one who showed him mercy." And Jesus said to him, "You go, and do likewise."[21]

Christ revealed in this passage that compassion and mercy are not exclusive to one's own people and must be shown to everyone, regardless of their backgrounds, reputations, nationalities, or beliefs. Christ lived this out, even while breaking Jewish cultural traditions, by speaking to prostitutes, tax collectors, and lepers. Christ gave the example for Christian leaders to follow, not only by having compassion for those in need, but also by showing mercy in meeting their needs. The Christian leader should be known by his compassion and mercy toward others. Although organizational leaders bear the difficult tasks of accountability through reprimands and firing, they must be able to show compassion to anyone under their care who is suffering. Leaders who see employees simply as a means to a financial end will benefit only themselves, failing to meet the needs of others in their care. Michael writes,

> A strong leader who is committed to providing the best possible Christian leadership will demonstrate a balance between personal toughness and pastoral tenderness. He is able to show sensitive compassion to his followers. Compassion might seem to be a weak leadership trait to those secular critics who believe that there is no substitute for tough leadership if one desires to be effective. Their view includes the traditional notion that macho authoritarian leaders personify the survival of the fittest, winner-take-all in a dog-eat-dog world.[22]

Jesus Christ, the strongest man to walk the face of the earth, also lived a life of compassion and mercy by setting the example for his followers to pursue.

---

21. Luke 10:30–37.
22. Michael, *Spurgeon on Leadership*, 153.

Four C's of Christocentric Leadership

In the postmodern world, although leading with compassion toward all who are in need may not fit the prevailing utilitarian mold of leadership, it is nonetheless the true way to lead, according to the Bible. The Apostle Paul provides the biblical application and reasoning for compassion:

> Blessed be the God and Father of our Lord Jesus Christ, the Father of mercies and God of all comfort, who comforts us in all our affliction, so that we may be able to comfort those who are in any affliction, with the comfort with which we ourselves are comforted by God. For as we share abundantly in Christ's sufferings, so through Christ we share abundantly in comfort too. If we are afflicted, it is for your comfort and salvation; and if we are comforted, it is for your comfort, which you experience when you patiently endure the same sufferings that we suffer.[23]

Paul shows the design of God in how he comforts (shows compassion and mercy toward) people so they, in turn, would do so to others. Those who have been afflicted can empathize with those who are dealing with the same trial and provide them the comfort given to them by God during their hardship. A remarkable example of this form of compassion is greatly displayed in the life of Joni Eareckson Tada, who developed quadriplegia as a result of a diving accident in 1967. Tada went through all the pain, emotions, and despair of anyone dealing with this type of catastrophe, but through God's mercy, she is using the rest of her life to reach other disabled people with the gospel of Jesus Christ. She provides encouragement to others with disabilities while meeting their physical needs with specialized wheelchairs.[24] Just as exemplified in the life of Joni Eareckson Tada, Christian leaders have both the duty and the honor to show compassion and mercy with the grace and riches provided to them by the Savior.

---

23. 2 Cor 1:3–7.
24. Joni and Friends, "Joni's Bio."

9

Servanthood

The Nemesis of Postmodernity

It shall not be so among you. But whoever would be great among you must be your servant, and whoever would be first among you must be your slave, even as the Son of Man came not to be served but to serve, and to give his life as a ransom for many.

—MATTHEW 20:26–28

IN POSTMODERN TIMES, THE emphasis on "I," "me," and "my" is central to decision-making and has left its mark on leadership theory. The age of social media has only emboldened the idea that each person is at the center of his own universe. Millions each day tweet or post their every move on Facebook, assuming that the masses are genuinely interested in every meal they eat or that they wish to see a myriad of photos from last evening's party. This virtual world has created a false reality and may be giving false hope to many. While postmoderns are typically codependent and thrive on the need for acceptance, validation, and attention, there is never enough to be found, leaving an emptiness many try to fill online through what the virtual world calls "friends." These "friends" are simply those who decided to hit a button to connect with someone else whom they may have never met in person. As quickly as these "friends" exist, they can be "deleted" (or better yet, "unfriended") without even an argument or discussion. Although this age is highly relational, the idea of serving others before oneself is not typically found in the vernacular. The virtual world has allowed the resistance to authority and the repudiation of societal norms to take hold as every "user" has a voice in this world with no accountability or filtering. Postmodernist Arthur Kroker believes the current mood of the postmodern culture is panic, which he describes as a "free fall."[1] Kroker maintains that this free fall comes from "the disappearance of *external* standards of public conduct... and the dissolution of the *internal* foundations of identity ... The self is transformed into an empty screen [notice the metaphor] of an exhausted, but hyper-technical culture."[2] This "free fall" is apparent when observing postmoderns in their continual quest to understand who they are in light of their ever-changing, on-screen avatar. Changing this inward mentality will be a major venture as it has become very engrained in the postmodern culture. Servant leadership, although antithetical to the postmodern era, provides a genuine example and opportunity to move people away from self-worship in their virtual world to serving others in the real world.

Oddly enough, a bridge exists between postmodern thought and servant leadership, which is worthy of pursuit. Paulien provides a measure of optimism for reaching the postmodern generation:

> Living in an age in which image is king, postmodern individuals place a high premium of humility, honesty, and authenticity in interpersonal relationships. They feel it is better to be honest about one's weaknesses and handicaps than to craft an image or "play the audience" ... Postmoderns not only have a strong sense of brokenness; they are willing to share that brokenness honestly with friends they consider safe. Humility and authenticity are, of course, very central attributes of genuine Christian faith.[3]

Christian leaders have an excellent opportunity to fill the void of humility and authenticity by answering the question of their origin. Christians should have the best answers for the postmodern generation as it eagerly desires something of substance but lacks sufficient examples in society. Postmoderns are very "spiritual," even though they deny the existence of a triune God with an exclusive message of truth. The Apostle Paul handled this predicament both humbly and confidently, while presenting objective

---

1. Veith, *Postmodern Times*, 82.
2. Ibid.
3. Paulien, *Everlasting Gospel*, 58

truth to the Jews and philosophers at Mars Hill. Paul ventured into a part of town where people debated deities, discussed ethics, and sought a higher level of knowledge. Paul, an educated man in his own right, used this opportunity to answer the questions often posed by this eclectic group:

> Now while Paul was waiting for them at Athens, his spirit was provoked within him as he saw that the city was full of idols. So he reasoned in the synagogue with the Jews and the devout persons, and in the marketplace every day with those who happened to be there. Some of the Epicurean and Stoic philosophers also conversed with him . . . So Paul, standing in the midst of the Areopagus, said: "Men of Athens, I perceive that in every way you are very religious. For as I passed along and observed the objects of your worship, I found also an altar with this inscription: 'To the unknown god.' What therefore you worship as unknown, this I proclaim to you. The God who made the world and everything in it, being Lord of heaven and earth, does not live in temples made by man, nor is he served by human hands, as though he needed anything, since he himself gives to all mankind life and breath and everything. And he made from one man every nation of mankind to live on all the face of the earth, having determined allotted periods and the boundaries of their dwelling place, that they should seek God, and perhaps feel their way toward him and find him. Yet he is actually not far from each one of us, for 'In him we live and move and have our being'; as even some of your own poets have said, 'For we are indeed his offspring.' Being then God's offspring, we ought not to think that the divine being is like gold or silver or stone, an image formed by the art and imagination of man." Now when they heard of the resurrection of the dead, some mocked. But others said, 'We will hear you again about this.'[4]

Paul's usual audience was the Jewish people, of which he was one. This group, like the postmoderns, designed their own truths and answers to the questions to the purpose of life. Just as is prevalent in the postmodern era, those with the greatest charisma and intellect were the voices of change. Although Paul was a very intelligent man (Acts 22), he was not known for his charismatic appeal. The greatest tool in Paul's arsenal was divine truth, acquired directly from Jesus Christ, with a mandate to use it at every opportunity. As the Areopagus sought to understand their unknown god, Paul presented the God who could be known in Jesus Christ. Paul's courage to obliterate their religious and philosophical systems would have

4. Acts 17:16–18, 22–32.

proved disastrous for him had he not provided a more plausible answer. Paul gained credibility with this audience, showing his understanding of their beliefs by taking them from the known to the unknown. Christian leaders can emulate Paul in the same way by meeting postmodern seekers where they are and leading them to the only path which will provide substantive answers to their inquiries. The outcome Paul received can also be expected of today's leaders: some will believe, some will mock, and others will wish to hear more. This is an encouraging conclusion to this passage as the Christian leader understands that the perfect presentation of truth does not guarantee acceptance and may result in mockery and resentment. However, the leader's conscience can be clear, knowing that he presented the unvarnished truth of Christ. Unlike some popular beliefs among Christians, someone cannot convince another person to believe, as regeneration is the ministry of the Holy Spirit (Eph 1, Rom 8–9).

Servant leadership has been a major focus of study since Robert Greenleaf coined the phrase in 1970.[5] While servant leadership has become an oft-used phrase over the past few decades, few know the story which moved Greenleaf to pursue this field of study. Greenleaf explains,

> The idea of the servant as leader came out of reading Hermann Hesse's *Journey to the East*. In this story we see a band of men on a mythical journey, probably also Hesse's own journey. The central figure of the story is Leo, who accompanies the party as the servant who does their menial chores, but who also sustains them with his spirit and his song. He is a person of extraordinary presence. All goes well until Leo disappears. Then the group falls into disarray and the journey is abandoned. They cannot make it without the servant Leo. The narrator, one of the party, after some years of wandering, finds Leo and is taken into the Order that had sponsored the journey. There he discovers that Leo, whom he had known first as servant, was in fact the titular head of the Order, its guiding spirit, a great and noble leader.[6]

Although Greenleaf's motivation for his journey into servant leadership was prompted by a mythological narrative, the originating idea is divine and presented throughout the canon of Scripture. However, Greenleaf also considered the overriding theme of service and servant leadership throughout the Bible when he wrote the following:

---

5. Greenleaf, *Servant as Leader*, 1.
6. Ibid.

> The idea of "servant" is deep in our Judeo-Christian heritage. The Concordance to the Standard Revised Version of the Bible lists over 1300 references to servant (including serve and service). Yet, after all of these millennia, there is ample evidence that ours is a low-caring society when judged by what is reasonable and possible with the resources at hand. There are many notable servants among us, but they sometimes seem to be losing ground to the neutral or nonserving people. It is argued that the outlook for our civilization at this moment is not promising, probably because not enough of us care enough for our fellow humans.[7]

Greenleaf's theory, although more secular than theological, began a very important discussion on a countercultural form of leadership which many consider contradictory, though others can appreciate its paradoxical nature. To develop the concept of the servant leader, it is wise to seek and understand its roots in biblical Christianity. For this purpose, several biblical features will be considered, including the aspects of redemption, compassionate love, stewardship, and the individual characteristics of biblical servant leadership.

Redemption

From the beginning, God has always called and commanded people to serve two entities: God and others. Nowhere in the Bible can one find an imperative to love, serve, worship, praise, or honor oneself. God illustrated this notion perfectly in the life, death, and resurrection of Jesus Christ. Even Christ did not seek his own will, but that of his Father (John 6:38). It is often noted that leaders should not give work to others which they are not willing to do themselves. Jesus Christ, sacrificially giving his life in an excruciating death, provided the ultimate example of servant leadership. This redemptive act of Christ is at the core of servant leadership, as expressed by Regent University Professor Dr. Joseph Bucci:

> Our knowledge of redemption is contextualized in the redemptive work of Christ on the Cross, and the expression of this transformed life seems more familiar to congregational life in a church setting, or through a personal interaction when seeking restoration among individuals ... Yet the call for transformation made by Jesus was conducted not only in religious settings, but more often

---

7. Greenleaf, *Servant Leadership*, 22.

in the marketplace among tradespersons. After all, much of the New Testament was written by marketplace leaders like the doctor Luke, the tax official Matthew, the tentmaker Paul and the owners of a fishing business (Peter, James and John) . . . It is a natural extension of this practice that a valid and valuable effort be made by faith-based leaders both within and outside of the church to follow the pattern of Jesus by forgiving and serving individuals with weaknesses, by seeking to restore them to useful contributions to the work of the kingdom of God and to future success in life.[8]

Since Greenleaf, many have contributed thoughtful works on the subject of servant leadership. Bucci's research revealed thirty-seven different models of servant leadership with three hundred eighty-one different dimensions, and of these works, only fifteen could be classified as faith-based.[9] Each of these models present a unique angle of the servant model, while Bucci's work ventures into new waters by exposing the redemptive aspect of servant leadership. The forgiveness and restorative features of the redemptive model are critical in understanding the "ransom" facet of Christ's words as penned in the Matthean pericope above. The redemptive focus answers the question of "why lead?" in this fashion, while also exposing the underlying motive in redemption. Leaders who are seeking to be Christ-like will not discard the weak and lowly, but will work to forgive, strengthen, and restore the down-and-out brother or sister. Though persons crushed by hardships may be the least likely to help others, they actually provide the greatest opportunity for serving, as reciprocation can be removed from the motive. After the Pharisees sought to trap Jesus by asking him about his association with tax collectors and sinners, Christ responds, "Those who are well have no need of a physician, but those who are sick. Go and learn what this means: 'I desire mercy, and not sacrifice. For I came not to call the righteous, but sinners.'"[10] If Christ's work or redemption reached down to those considered the "wretches" of society, does the Christian leader have a mandate to do otherwise?

---

8. Bucci, *Redemptive Managerial Dimensions*, 14.
9. Ibid.
10. Matt 9:12-13.

The Leadership Imperative

Compassionate Love

As discussed in chapter 5, it is *agape* love, or love's highest form, which leads one to have a desire to serve another. The natural or human tendency for humanity is to serve self. If one documents every action throughout a given day, the tally will likely show that most actions were accomplished based on self-interests. Part of humanity's sin nature, adopted in the fall of man, is pride and a desire to live for self-gratification. To move out of this state, one must desire something else more than self. Christians, at the time of regeneration, are given a new heart, along with a desire for God and his written word. In the Old Testament, Ezekiel spoke of the change which occurs once one believes: "A new heart also will I give you, and a new spirit will I put within you: and I will take away the stony heart out of your flesh, and I will give you an heart of flesh. And I will put my spirit within you, and cause you to walk in my statutes, and ye shall keep my judgments, and do them,"[11] while in the New Testament the Apostle Paul proclaims, "if anyone is in Christ, he is a new creation. The old has passed away; behold, the new has come."[12] The transformation which occurs at the moment of salvation is efficacious and leads one to love God and serve others. Van Dierendonck and Patterson call this source "compassionate love" in their servant leadership model, with the following explanation:

> The first four characteristics (empowerment, stewardship, authenticity and providing direction) are placed together as exemplifying the core of servant leadership behavior. We suggest that humility may be better conceptualized as a virtuous attitude that underlies servant leadership behavior toward followers and that two elements can be distinguished within interpersonal acceptance: forgiveness and compassionate love. Compassionate love is placed in our model as underlying a servant leader's need to serve, and forgiveness is placed with humility as one of four virtuous attitudes (See Figure 3).[13]

Figure 3

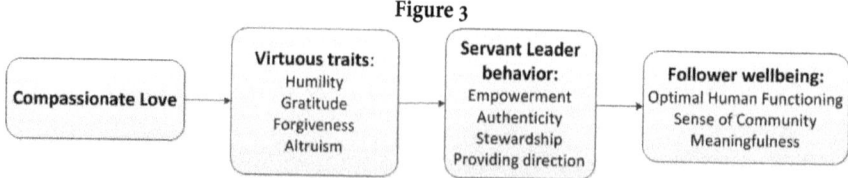

---

11. Ezek 36:26–27 (KJV).
12. 2 Cor 5:17.
13. van Dierendonck and Patterson, "Compassionate Love," 120.

This figure presents a simple yet profound progression from "compassionate love" to "follower well-being," based on the noted traits and behavior. This model aligns with the Scriptures, as it never leads back to self or self-interests, but instead maintains the focus on the follower and how he may be best served. Van Dierendonck and Patterson continue this thought and add the macro benefit to the entity which they serve:

> Compassionate love is harmonious with servant leadership to the extent that servant leaders must have such great love for the followers that they are willing to learn the gifts and talents of each one of the followers. The leader that leads with compassionate love has a focus on the employee first, then on the talents of the employee, and lastly on how this benefits the organization.[14]

The supremacy of *agape*, or compassionate, love cannot be understated, as it is indelibly present in the foundation in any Christological servant-leader model.

Stewardship

As one considers the concept of stewardship, the Genesis creation account may come to mind, for God commanded Adam and Eve to manage the new creation (Gen 2). The Apostle Paul considered himself a steward of the mysteries of God, or the gospel of Christ (1 Cor 4:1). In each of these accounts of stewardship, God was entrusting something to his people to wisely care for and to nurture. Mohler approaches servant leadership in the context of stewardship:

> The biblical concept of a steward is simple. A steward is someone who manages and leads what is not his own, and he leads knowing that he will give an account to the Lord as the owner and ruler of all. Stewards are entrusted with responsibility. Indeed, stewards in the Bible are shown to have both great authority and great responsibility. Kings had stewards who administered their kingdoms—just think of Joseph as Pharoah's steward in Egypt. Rich citizens hired stewards to serve as what amounted to chief executive officers of their enterprises—consider the parable Jesus told about the wicked steward in Luke 16:1-8 ... Clearly, this is a concept that is central to both Christian discipleship and Christian leadership. Christian leaders are invested with a stewardship of influence,

---

14. Ibid, 121.

authority, and trust that we are called to fulfill. In one sense this underlines just how much God entrusts to his human creatures, fallible and frail as we are. We are called to exercise dominion over creation, but not as ones who own what we are called to lead. Our assignment is to serve on behalf of another.[15]

Christian leaders are stewards of the people God calls them to lead, which further elevates one's level of responsibility. When a leader contemplates the gravity of this duty, he must humbly approach each situation as a path to lead one to God's plan lest he lead one astray. Leaders are looked upon for guidance, clarity, truth, wisdom, and counsel; they must approach each with grace, humility, and patience. Per an Old Testament explanation of stewardship,

> The steward of the Old Testament was depicted as a servant, but not merely as a slave. Such a person was a foreman or supervisor of sorts, responsible for making appropriate decisions, giving orders and generally managing the household. Holding such a position implied a certain relationship of trust and shared responsibility between the steward and the owner of the household.[16]

This illustration provides a fitting correlation between the owner of the household being God and the servants being the leaders, called of God, to manage affairs. Of Christ, Botha notes:

> In the New Testament, Jesus Christ displays a new societal model of stewardship through his devotion and righteousness. Jesus never considered himself the focal point of his work. He was obedient to his master and responsible for his master's interests on earth. Traditional theology paints Jesus Christ as king, priest and prophet, but practical theology awards us the freedom to consider also the example that Jesus set as a steward.[17]

Sendjaya and Sarros develop this further: "A profound example of such secure servant leaders again is Jesus Christ himself, who 'did not consider equality with God something to be grasped, but made Himself nothing, taking the very nature of a servant' (Phil 2:3–8)."[18] Commenting on the story of the foot-washing incident, Ford points out that it was not weakness

---

15. Mohler, *Conviction to Lead*, 136.
16. Botha, "Teaching as an Act of Stewardship," 1, 3.
17. Ibid.
18. Sendjaya Sarros, "Servant Leadership," 61.

which compelled Jesus to be a servant in this case. Rather, it was Jesus' strong self-image which moved him to make a voluntary offering of himself; he "operated out of a sense of being deeply secure in his identity."[19] This point is important to note in a culture which deems servanthood as a weak and lowly position. As personified as "lions" and "lambs," the Bible depicts one with great strength (a leader) alongside the meek and mild (a follower). Consequently, the steward model is fitting and useful in the continuing dialogue on servant leadership.

Attributes, Principles, and Distinctives

As previously mentioned, hundreds of dimensions, roles, attributes, and distinctives have been discovered relating to servant leadership. While articles and books may be written using the terms servant leadership or Christian leadership, it is important to use discernment to ensure their claims align with the Scriptures. Bucci has presented several models that provide compelling alignments with the Bible, including the following lists of servant characteristics:

The Ten Facets of Servant Leadership (Rardin)

Scripture References: Matthew, Mark, and others

Characteristics/Attributes:

1. Focuses on the individual
2. Empathic
3. Caring
4. Self-sacrificing
5. Nurturing
6. Stoops
7. Submits to gifts of others
8. Saves
9. Full of grace

---

19. Ford, *Transforming Leadership*, 153.

10. Humbly serves the purpose of God in the lives of others[20]

Unique to Rardin's facets of servant leadership are the traits of stooping, submitting, saving, showing grace, and humbly serving for the glory of God. These five elements are inherently scriptural and are unlikely to be found in secular writings on this subject. Secular works often present characteristics that would align with the Bible, but the motive behind them is quite different. It would be a challenge to integrate these five traits by Rardin into secular works, as they completely remove the element of self and reciprocity. Especially noteworthy is the notion of submitting to the gifts of others. Leaders can easily become convinced that they hold all the answers and "know all things." This is true of no human being, and wisdom dictates that the leader yield to those with more expertise in each area and also to encourage them to grow in their field of giftedness. The Scriptures provide clarity on mutual submission, as the Apostle Paul commands the believers in Ephesus to submit to each other "out of reverence for Christ."[21]

Summary of Principles—A Servant Leader Does These Things (Sullivan)

Scripture References: Matt 20:28, Mark 10:42–45, and others

Characteristics/Attributes:

1. Showing compassion (representing patience and focus on the individual)
2. Demonstrating humility
3. Remaining impartial
4. Living a life of integrity
5. Building trust by being trustworthy
6. Applying knowledge and experience while developing wisdom[22]

One important distinction in Sullivan's list is "applying knowledge and experience while developing wisdom." The book of Proverbs incessantly focuses on wisdom and knowledge as the key to success in life. It is important

---

20. Rardin, *The Servant's Guide to Leadership*.
21. Eph 5:21.
22. Sullivan, *Servant First!*

to note that wisdom must accompany knowledge for it to be fruitful. As the Scriptures provide the only seamless basis for true knowledge and wisdom, they should be consulted in every realm of study, especially leadership theory. Solomon's opening salvo to this wisdom literature reads,

> The proverbs of Solomon, son of David, king of Israel:
> To know wisdom and instruction,
> > to understand words of insight,
> > to receive instruction in wise dealing,
> > in righteousness, justice, and equity;
> > to give prudence to the simple,
> > knowledge and discretion to the youth.
> Let the wise hear and increase in learning,
> > and the one who understands obtain guidance,
> > to understand a proverb and a saying,
> > the words of the wise and their riddles.
> The fear of the Lord is the beginning of knowledge;
> > fools despise wisdom and instruction.[23]

Solomon moves through the rest of his writings with the desire to instill godly principles; the foolish must become wise, and the wise must grow in wisdom. Throughout the wisdom literature, Solomon gives dire warnings of devastating repercussions to those who venture onto the path of foolishness:

> Because I have called and you refused to listen,
> > have stretched out my hand and no one has heeded,
> because you have ignored all my counsel
> > and would have none of my reproof,
> I also will laugh at your calamity;
> > I will mock when terror strikes you,
> when terror strikes you like a storm
> > and your calamity comes like a whirlwind,
> > when distress and anguish come upon you.
> Then they will call upon me, but I will not answer;
> > they will seek me diligently but will not find me.
> Because they hated knowledge
> > and did not choose the fear of the Lord.[24]

Conversely, for those choosing the path of wisdom, Solomon proclaims, "but whoever listens to me will dwell secure and will be at ease, without

---

23. Prov 1:1–7.
24. Prov 1:24–29.

dread of disaster."²⁵ The inclusion of wisdom and knowledge in Sullivan's principles is far more than a nicety; it is a necessity to servant leadership.

Seven Distinctives of Servant Leadership (DelHousaya and Brewer)

Scripture References: Matthew, John, and others

Characteristics/Attributes:

1. A servant leader knows their person [power].
2. A servant leader knows their position [authority].
3. A servant leader knows their purpose [rule].
4. A servant leader knows their provision [headship].
5. A servant leader knows their perception [example].
6. A servant leader knows their profession [servant].
7. A servant leader knows their preference [humility].²⁶

DelHousaya and Brewer pursue the aspect of competence in knowing who they are in relation to each of their responsibilities and traits. This list of distinctives differs from other lists, as it attempts to balance the strong traits leaders so often trip over (power, authority, rule, and headship) with the servant requisites of example, service, and humility. This list is useful in prompting the leader to remember who he is in all his roles and responsibilities while ensuring he does not use his power to crush his followers. When the mother of John and James requested that her sons be elevated above others in the kingdom, Jesus offered this stern rebuke:

> You know that the rulers of the Gentiles lord it over them, and their great ones exercise authority over them. It shall not be so among you. But whoever would be great among you must be your servant, and whoever would be first among you must be your slave, even as the Son of Man came not to be served but to serve, and to give his life as a ransom for many.²⁷

---

25. Prov 1:33.
26. DelHousaya and Brewer, *Servant Leadership*.
27. Matt 20:25b–28.

Servanthood

Christian leaders must maintain a balanced perspective of the power that they hold while being careful to exercise it with grace. While the prospect of "lording" power over others may be productive in the short term, the long-term result will be mistrust, anger, and resentment.

Leadership by the Book—Summary of Servant Leadership Principles (Blanchard, Hybels, and Hodges)

Scripture References: Matt 20:28, Mark 10:42–45, and others

Characteristics/Attributes:

1. Effective leadership starts on the inside.
2. Real change in behavior requires a real change of the heart.
3. True leadership starts on the inside with a servant heart, then moves outward to serve others.
4. I take on the challenge of leadership when I see it as a way in which I can serve others.
5. My main interest is the development and care for those I lead.
6. I want to be held accountable for my leadership performance.
7. I am willing to listen; and, in actuality, I enjoy receiving feedback to help me improve my leadership.
8. Leaders are not meant to be served, but to serve others.
9. I praise the progress of my people; I look to catch them doing something right.
10. Servant leadership is not about pleasing everyone, but pleasing God first, developing people second, attaining the company's mission, and finally finding satisfaction in achieving all three.
11. Effective leaders have a support/accountability group to keep them on track.
12. Leaders regularly make an inventory of their actions, motives and thoughts, to be sure that they are consistent with the servant leadership model.[28]

---

28. Blanchard et al., *Leadership by the Book*.

Blanchard, Hybels, and Hodges take a soundly visceral approach to servant leadership by emphasizing the "heart," "inside," "motives," and "thoughts" of the leader. This style disqualifies leaders with a proclivity toward self-motivation and mutuality as the intent is focused exclusively on the receiver. The supercilious leader may give the outward appearance of having servant leader traits, but will eventually be exposed due to his pretentious actions. Greenleaf presented this distinction early in his writings:

> Becoming a servant-leader begins with the natural feeling that one wants to serve, to serve first. Then conscious choice brings one to aspire to lead. That person is sharply different from one who is leader first, perhaps because of the need to assuage an unusual power drive or to acquire material possessions. For such people, it will be a later choice to serve—after leadership is established. The leader-first and the servant-first are two extreme types. Between them are the shadings and blends that are part of the infinite variety of human nature.[29]

Although Greenleaf avoids the source of this desire (God), he rightly describes the desire as coming from within and needing to be acted upon by "choice." He also draws a dissimilarity in motive between the servant leader and the leader with less than stellar motives. Christ's imperative reveals this distinction in motive and the outcome:

> Do not lay up for yourselves treasures on earth, where moth and rust destroy and where thieves break in and steal, but lay up for yourselves treasures in heaven, where neither moth nor rust destroys and where thieves do not break in and steal. For where your treasure is, there your heart will be also.[30]

The Christian leader will treasure the opportunity to honor God by serving man. This has lasting results for both the giver and the receiver of the blessing.

Servant leadership theory continues to bloom as research transitions from the qualitative to the quantitative arena in search of efficacy and validation. According to Berger,

> Servant Leadership has emerged from four decades of dialogue, empirical research, and anecdotal evidence with the proven potential to make a profound impact on people, organizations, and

---

29. Spears and Lawrence, *Practicing Servant-Leadership*, 5.
30. Matt 6:19–21.

society. The fundamental issue servant leadership scholars must address in the fifth decade of servant leadership research remains the development of strong theory.[31]

Few will write against servant leadership theory due to its popularity and basis in humility. However, many will refrain from embracing it, for as the "others-focus" fails to fill the human ego. Leaders with lofty goals of power, wealth, and hierarchical authority will find little value in servant leadership as the outcome may not lead to these conclusions. Over the last two decades, many corporate catastrophes like Tyco, Enron, Worldcom, Healthsouth, Freddie Mac, Lehman Brothers, and Bernard L. Madoff Investment Securities could have been prevented if the leadership teams had embraced servant leadership. If these businesses had not failed, thousands of employees and billions of dollars in investments could have been spared. Van Dierendonck identified servant leadership as a possible solution to the paucity of ethics in the business community and as a potential tool by which to increase employee engagement.[32] While servant leadership theory requires more academic research, few would argue that traits such as honesty, humility, grace, empathy, and love could cause any problems. Servant leadership has the power to completely transform an organization.

---

31. Berger, "Servant Leadership 2.0," 146.
32. van Dierendonck, "Servant Leadership."

10

Communicating with Clarity in an Era of Fluidity

> *Words are the priceless currency of communication. The most effective leaders are collectors and connoisseurs of words. They polish and perfect the deployment of specific words for greatest effect. They know that words are powerful when memorable and delivered with conviction. They know that Mark Twain was right when he said that the difference between the almost right word and the right word is "the difference between the lightning bug and the lightning."*
>
> —ALBERT MOHLER[1]

The Transformative Nature of Postmodern Communication

THE WAY PEOPLE COMMUNICATE has changed significantly since the advent of the internet, social media, and smartphone technologies. Leaders in this new world of electronic communication struggle with limited attention spans, massive data availability, and privacy issues. Traditional modes of communication, such as print media, are quickly becoming obsolete as new media with its 24/7 capabilities consume the minds of the masses.

---

1. Mohler, *Conviction*, 92.

Communicating with Clarity in an Era of Fluidity

Kuran writes, "We face an era of information overload and attention deficit. Information is increasingly free, and therefore diminishing in value—unless infused with true meaning. Computers work great with numbers, but they cannot manage the meaning-making process."[2] Instead of handwritten letters and phone calls, the preferred methods of communication now entail texting, Facebook posts, tweeting, and Instagram. Ironically, even email use among the younger generation is losing ground as the "instant" styles provide quicker gratification. As an example, if someone is celebrating a birthday, photos of the occasion are taken with a smartphone and posted on Instagram; relatives living in Germany can view these pictures within seconds. These relatives can post them to their Facebook accounts where hundreds of friends can view them and post their thoughts on the message board. All of this can occur in just a couple of minutes. Likewise, a terrorist attack can happen in Turkey at 10:00 AM, and the majority of the world will be alerted by 10:05 AM with graphic photos available at 10:07 AM.

The postmodern era is moving at lightning speed, requiring leaders to think, react, and communicate faster than ever before. On the positive side, leaders have access to much larger audiences than in any time in history. MacArthur illustrates this point by showing how the last century has changed the reach of the gospel:

> No previous generation has been blessed with the means of mass communication like ours. A hundred years ago, "Christian communication" consisted almost totally of preaching sermons and writing books. The only form of mass communication was the press. It never occurred to men like Charles Spurgeon that the means would exist to transmit live sounds and images via satellite to every nation in the world. Spurgeon was the most listened-to preacher in history by the end of the nineteenth century. He preached to huge crowds in his church. By some estimates, four million people actually heard him preach over a remarkable lifetime of ministry. But today, via radio, Chuck Swindoll preaches to more people than that in a typical week. J. Vernon McGee ("he being dead yet speaketh") has been broadcasting every weekday worldwide for decades. If you count the sermons that are translated and preached in other languages, McGee has undoubtedly preached to more people than any other person in history—and he continues to do so from the grave.[3]

2. Kuran, "Leader as Storyteller," 121.
3. MacArthur, "A Challenge," 7.

Christian leaders must address these changes of communication modes and styles in order to effectively lead in the postmodern era. Although the means of communication may be adapted, the message must never be watered down or weakened. In fact, leaders can use this era to restore the need for deeper thinking and contextualization, which is very difficult to accomplish in two hundred eighty characters. The blessing of the current era is the ubiquitous ways leaders can present messages, including blogs, vlogs, websites, and audio books. The curse of the current era is the lack of attention spans among the hearers or readers who are only interested in the headlines or the highlights. Christian leaders are communicators who must be skilled orators and writers, just as the prophets and saints of old. Although the methods of communication have changed, the need for sound instruction remains. MacArthur wisely notes,

> As Christian writers and communicators, I challenge you to forget what is fashionable and concern yourself with what is true. Do not be quick to embrace the trends of modern marketing. Certainly we should use the new media. But rather than adapting our message to suit the medium, let's use the medium to present the message as clearly, as accurately, and as fully as possible. If we are faithful in that, the soil God has prepared will bear fruit. His Word will not return void.[4]

Authentic Christian leaders, communicating with conviction while taking advantage of new mediums, will take the gospel message to the world like never before.

The Scriptures often speak of using wise principles to communicate. As communicators of God's truth to a fallen world, Christian leaders have the responsibility to write and express themselves in a way which honors God and edifies humanity. Many passages reveal the way Christians should communicate in a God honoring way. Some of these include,

- Let no corrupting talk come out of your mouths, but only such as is good for building up, as fits the occasion, that it may give grace to those who hear.[5]

- A word fitly spoken is like apples of gold in a setting of silver.[6]

---

4. Ibid., 15.
5. Eph 4:29.
6. Prov 25:11.

Communicating with Clarity in an Era of Fluidity

- Let the words of my mouth and the meditation of my heart be acceptable in your sight, O Lord, my rock and my redeemer.[7]
- Listen to advice and accept instruction, and in the end you will be wise.[8]
- Everyone should be quick to listen, slow to speak, and slow to become angry.[9]
- When words are many, sin is not absent, but he who holds his tongue is wise.[10]
- Reckless words pierce like a sword, but the tongue of the wise brings healing.[11]
- A gentle answer turns away wrath, but a harsh word stirs up anger.[12]
- Kings take pleasure in honest lips; they value a man who speaks the truth.[13]
- Speaking the truth in love, we will in all things grow up into him who is the Head, that is, Christ.[14]
- For out of the overflow of the heart the mouth speaks.[15]

These passages provide a moral framework from which to communicate. Because the Scriptures do not address or limit the types of communication methods, great freedom is available for leaders to use new approaches as long as they uphold the divine, moral standards of communication as detailed in the God's word.

Leader as Storyteller

Gaining and maintaining the attention and interest of others is integral to leadership success. A leader with the greatest ideas, goals, and aspirations is

7. Ps 19:14.
8. Prov 19:20.
9. Jas 1:19.
10. Prov 10:19.
11. Prov 12:18.
12. Prov 15:1.
13. Prov 16:13.
14. Eph 4:15–16.
15. Matt 12:34.

only as good as his ability to effectively communicate them to others. While communication is a multi-faceted field of study and has been researched intently over many decades, the simple act of telling a story has always been a valuable way to connect with others in an intuitive way. Kuran posits,

> We've arrived in a world where everyone is a content creator. Content is all about hard data. We should note that *research* shows it is 22 times more likely to remember a story than concrete data. Content goes to the left-brain, and the owner of the content is the leader. Quality content is never enough because it is determined by context. Finding, sorting, endorsing, sharing—it's the beginning of a new chapter. The follower is the owner of the context. That is why it is sustainable. We should marry content and context in a skillful way for impactful storytelling.[16]

Stories have the ability to relate the listener to the topic with the intent of moving them to action. When a leader presents a story, the audience becomes part of the larger narrative and no longer sees itself as a spectator looking in from the outside.

Denning encapsulates the importance of using the art of storytelling to reach the desired goal with an audience:

> If leaders are to . . . succeed in inspiring enduring enthusiasm for more basic changes in more difficult audiences, they need to set aside any idea of imposing their will or moving their listeners to a predetermined position. The task is rather one of enabling the audience to see possibilities that they have hitherto missed. It means creating the capability in the audience to view for themselves the world and their relation with others in a new and more truthful light. It involves pointing a way forward for people to find themselves—for whatever reason—cornered by the current story that they are living. It entails enabling the audience to recognize a new, different, and more promising story that they could be living, which they for some reason have not visualized up until now.[17]

Politicians often frame arguments with stories meant to convince people to change their minds on a given topic in hopes of supporting a bill, a candidate, or a moral philosophy. Polletta presents the power of storytelling thusly:

---

16. Kuran, "Leader as Storyteller," 121.
17. Denning, *The Secret Language of Leadership*, 87.

The key to the power of narrative, researchers have shown, is that we hear stories differently than other kinds of messages. For a long time, scholars of persuasion thought we processed messages in one of two ways: "centrally," where we really scrutinize a message and evaluate its claims critically, or "peripherally," where we absorb a message casually, judging it less by its content than by the appeal of the speaker or our mood.[18]

Stories, therefore, can impact and move people through reason or emotion, ensuring that the spectrum of listeners can receive something convincing.

Successful organizations often use the story of their own heritages and humble beginnings to aid employees in developing respect for the history, founding leaders, and original goals of the entity. Establishing these roots through retelling the story makes people feel like they are part of something much larger than themselves. The Disney Corporation, for example, uses the goals of its founder, Walt Disney, to maintain a perspective based on founding principles. If an organization appreciates and has a sense of loyalty to its founding principles, it is more likely to retain its heritage, even during rapid growth. Baldoni provides sage advice for the organizational use of storytelling:

1. Identify the stories in your organization. What obstacles did your company overcome as it became what it is today? Specify the context and character of each.

2. Identify the legends in your organization. Why are they legends? What things did they accomplish? What leadership lessons can you draw from their example?

3. If your organization has been around for more than five years, make a practice of inviting veterans in your company to spend time with newcomers. Ask them to share stories of the old days so that new people can get a sense of time, place, and culture.

4. If your organization is a brand-new venture, make a practice of inviting members of the organization to share stories from their past experiences. Some of these accounts may prove insightful; others may not. By encouraging people to share stories, you are trying to gain insight into what worked, what didn't, and why.

18. Polletta, "Storytelling in Politics," 27.

5. Use stories as vision tools. Invite the group to imagine the future of the team, the department, or the organization. Choose a date at some point in the future—one year, two years, five years. Ask these questions to get people thinking and to create a visionary narrative: What will the new organization be like? Be as descriptive as possible. How will you be able to judge its success? What individuals (or teams) will others want to tell stories about? Why? (Be certain to ask someone to write the stories. Save them for future reference).[19]

When organizational leaders tell stories, they connect with their audiences in ways that statistics, charts, and graphs cannot. While becoming part of the narrative, the audience feels valued, appreciated, and part of the organizational strategy; this results in higher morale, improved retention, and greater output. Denning notes,

> Storytelling is a crucial tool for management and leadership, because often nothing else works. Charts leave listeners bemused. Prose remains unread. Dialogue is just too laborious and slow. Time after time, when faced with the task of persuading a group of managers or front-line staff in a large organization to get enthusiastic about a major change, storytelling is the only thing that works.[20]

While quantitative data is essential to tracking and understanding the production and economics of business, it can be best understood and appreciated when presented in story form, where the data and real-life synergize to form a purposeful narrative.

Christian leaders are familiar with the many narratives presented throughout Scripture, as these stories translate dilemmas from thousands of years ago into a contemporary context. Although cultural nuances and changes must be considered, the biblical narratives can be understood just as well today as in the biblical era. The Synoptic Gospels record thirty-nine parables presented by Christ to a multitude of audiences. According to Kistemaker,

> Parables in both Gospels are characterized by contrasts. All the parables demonstrate artistry in their unity, coherence, balance, contrast, recurrence, and symmetry. Jesus' repetition of similar parables on separate occasions illustrates His goal of giving emphasis by way of repetition. By using open-ended parables, Jesus

---

19. Baldoni, *Great Communication*, 184–85.
20. Denning, "Leadership Storytelling," para. 6.

drew His listeners into real-life situations and presented them with the need for a decision on their parts. Allegory in Jesus' parables brought people into familiar surroundings and highlighted the mercy of God toward sinners. All in all, the parables of Jesus were in a category all their own and were quite distinct from other parabolic teachings in their timelessness and universality.[21]

Jesus Christ used parables more than anyone else in Scripture. The word "parable" derives from the Greek words *para* (beside) and *ballo* (throw) with the literal meaning "to place alongside." It suggests a comparison between two things that are alike in some way.[22] For instance, Jesus compared various soils, wise and foolish servants, the rich man and Lazarus, sheep and goats, and wise and foolish virgins. These short narratives ensure that the hearer is identified as being in one camp or the other and that he understands the implication of being in either group. These powerful statements were presented to the masses but explained in depth to only the disciples. MacArthur describes the parables this way:

> Jesus' parables were ingeniously simple word pictures with profound spiritual lessons. His teaching was full of these everyday stories. Some of them were no more than fleeting remarks about commonplace incidents, objects, or persons. In fact, the most compact of all Jesus' short stories does not even complete a verse of Scripture. It is found in Matthew 13:33: "The kingdom of heaven is like leaven, which a woman took and hid in three measures of meal till it was all leavened."[23]

Jesus created the human mind and intimately understood that stories could reach man's heart and cognizance better than any other form of communication due to our deeply relational natures. Jesus was often questioned on weighty matters of the law, life, and salvation, and usually chose to tell a story in lieu of a direct answer, knowing that the narrative would be much more profound. It may, at times, be appropriate for Christian leaders to give quick answers to their employees' questions. However, in many cases, a personal narrative or another useful story will allow for a greater impact and a motive for positive change.

---

21. Kistemaker, "Jesus As Storyteller," 49.
22. MacArthur, *Parables: The Mysteries*, xxvi.
23. Ibid.

The Leadership Imperative

Leadership Types

The most dynamic leadership communication styles are both highly personal and relational, based on the essential element of establishing trust. Politicians struggle in this area, as surveys show that they are typically considered to be dishonest and untrustworthy. (A 2016 Gallup Poll revealed that only 42 percent of Americans trust in political leaders, which is down from 63 percent in 2004.)[24] With these ratings, politicians are working harder than ever to "relate" to their constituents. Candidates often rely on professionals to remake their images into something which aligns with current polling. In the 2016 presidential election, candidate Hillary Clinton made repeated attempts to revise, change, and improve her image to the American public. Unfortunately for Clinton, voters are increasingly looking for something authentic. Although voters were concerned with many aspects of Donald Trump's persona, he was able to win the electoral college because many Americans could relate to him and his "politically incorrect" personality. Trump broke the mold of the American politician, previously characterized as polished, pretty, and poll-tested. As presented earlier, postmoderns seek leaders to whom they can relate and who they see as authentic. Hardly a leadership communication book exists which would promote the style of Donald Trump as effective and persuasive, but he was dually effective in both areas.

Baldoni presents four leadership communication styles which are all effective in their powers of persuasion. These styles include Transformer, Visionary, Coach, and Expert (see Figure 4).[25]

Figure 4

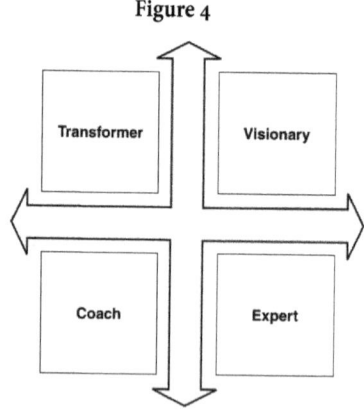

24. Jones, "Americans' Trust."
25. Baldoni, *Great Communication*, 16

Communicating with Clarity in an Era of Fluidity

Baldoni recognizes that a leader's public and private communication styles may differ, but also explains the need for leaders to communicate publicly:

> As a leadership communicator, you will be called upon to make your messages public. Why? Because that's how you lead. When a leader keeps everything inside, people are left to their own devices to try and figure out what the leader may, or may not, want. This is a failure of communications and a failure of leadership.[26]

Although Moses struggled with speech (possibly a stutter), God still called on him to communicate his will to the masses. Hence, each of Baldoni's communication styles is a design for both public and private leadership communication. The first of these styles, the "Expert," is the individual in the organization who sees the big picture as well as all the details at the micro level. In addition to understanding the organizational underpinnings, he can communicate it in a way that everyone can understand and enjoy. Military generals, such as Norman Schwarzkopf and Colin Powell, best fit this mold, due to their strategic, operational, and tactical understanding of warfare and their abilities to communicate it well to others. The second style, the "Visionary," "are those leaders whose ardent belief in their cause outweighs their words. Their speaking style comes from deep within, from their inner core values. Their mission is to persuade, to change points of view. Their leadership does not stop when the words do. Rather, it continues in the conduct of their daily lives."[27] A powerful example of a visionary leader is Martin Luther: one who toiled to reform the Christian church, returning it to its biblical roots. Luther's communication style arose from his passionate convictions; he was effective because he practiced what he preached. The third communication style, the "Transformer," is part visionary and part expert.[28] The late Steve Jobs, of Apple Inc., is a good example of a transformer style. He excelled as a technical expert in his field, but unlike many computer gurus, he was able to publicly communicate (or sell) his new ideas to prospective customers. Jobs did not simply update technology, he created technology which had not previously existed, while convincing millions that it would change their lives. Finally, the "Coach" style is described by Baldoni as:

---

26. Ibid., 16.
27. Ibid., 18.
28. Ibid., 19.

> A collaborator, the one who is called upon by virtue of her or his expertise on a particular subject. Coaches are those who change organizations one person at a time. They look for the unique way to communicate to an individual by discovering what motivates that person, e.g., more money, advancement, or prestige. Once the coach learns the motivational point, he or she can leverage it to help the person succeed.[29]

Baldoni used the example of the great Green Bay Packers coach Vince Lombardi to describe this communication style,

> Vince Lombardi was a coach who was able to communicate to players one at a time; his players say that he got them to play better because he raised their expectations of themselves. In other words, he elevated their own perceptions of their abilities and in so doing enabled them to play better. When Lombardi addressed the entire team, he leveraged the raised expectations to the whole team. But he did more: He provided a firm foundation. How? By teaching. Having begun his coaching career as a high school teacher, Lombardi continued his teaching of the fundamentals. His teaching gave the team a framework upon which they could apply their individual and collective talents.[30]

Lombardi's ability to effectively communicate and motivate each individual player created a heightened level of trust and loyalty in their esteemed coach; they played their best in an effort to please him.

Leader as Listener

By far, the most difficult part of the communication process is listening. Although communication requires a sender and a receiver, the latter has the more difficult role to play, as listening requires a proactive desire to hear and understand what is being stated. Leaders who struggle to listen are those who fail to understand the wants and needs of their respective followers. Furthermore, active listening bridges the potential trust gap between the sender and receiver, for listening shows that one cares or empathizes with the originator. The best leaders are those who thrive in a continual learning mode and wish to make decisions via the best information available. Listening, therefore, is a leadership necessity which best ensures

---

29. Ibid., 18.
30. Ibid., 19.

that new knowledge is received, understood, and acted upon. According to Bodie, "Listening is deeply rooted in the context of its ability to help, create, maintain and enhance positive interpersonal relationships. It is the quintessential positive interpersonal communication behavior as it connotes an appreciation of an interest in the other."[31] Although many volumes have been written on giving speeches, using persuasion techniques, and refining debating skills, the act of listening is just as important as executing a corporate presentation. Jack Welch stated it well: "Real communication is an attitude, an environment. It's the most interactive of all processes. It requires countless hours of eyeball-to-eyeball back and forth. It involves more listening than talking. It is a constant, interactive process aimed at [creating] consensus."[32] Welch rightly notes that communication is consistent and necessitates more listening than speaking.

Christian leaders seeking to meet the needs of others must first become trained listeners. As the servant leader's desire is to put others first by caring for them and meeting their needs, the leader must first listen to them before he can wisely respond. Northouse posits,

> Communication between leaders and followers is an interactive process which includes sending and receiving messages (i.e., talking and listening). Servant leaders communicate by listening first. They recognize listening is a learned discipline which involves hearing and being receptive to what others have to say. Through listening, servant leaders acknowledge the viewpoint of followers and validate these perspectives.[33]

Listening is a key aspect of servant leadership and can often be one of the most challenging to perfect. It is notable that out of Spears's ten critical characteristics of servant leaders (listening, empathy, healing, awareness, persuasion, conceptualisation, foresight, stewardship, commitment to the growth of people, and building community), listening is listed as first and foremost.[34] Just as listening is essential to servant leadership, it is also important that the followers know that their words are being heard and understood. The National Education Association provides some simple, yet useful tips regarding active listening:

---

31. Bodie, "The Active Empathic Listening," 59.
32. Baldoni, *Great Communication*, 118.
33. Northouse, *Leadership*, 221.
34. Spears, "Character," 25.

A poor listener:

- Interrupts the speaker
- Thinks only about what he or she is going to say next
- Looks away from the person speaking
- Pays attention to other things going on
- Makes side comments to others

A good listener:

- Focuses on the person talking and allows him or her to finish talking
- Looks at the other person: to indicate readiness to listen, and to observe the person's body language to learn more about how the speaker is feeling
- Gives nonverbal signals to show he or she is listening: a nod, smile, or frown, for example
- Uses verbal signals to show interest in what the speaker is saying or to give feedback with phrases such as
    - "Uh huh" or "I didn't know that" (showing encouragement)
    - "I'm not sure what you mean" (asking for clarification)
    - "You said that . . ." or "If I understand you correctly . . ." (showing an understanding of what the speaker said)
- Tries to use the same energy and emotional level as the speaker, to show an understanding of what the speaker is feeling[35]

For the Christian leader, listening is an active part of faith, for the Scriptures often command us to listen and to hear the message. The Apostle Paul writes, "So faith comes from hearing, and hearing through the word of Christ."[36] Solomon exhorted, "A wise man will hear and increase in learning, And a man of understanding will acquire wise counsel."[37] Jesus said, "Listen

---

35. National Education Association, "Build Better Listening Skills."
36. Rom 10:17.
37. Prov 1:5.

to Me, all of you, and understand."[38] Just as Christian leaders must continually listen to and hear the voice of God through his written word, they must also listen to the wishes of others to best serve them. Johansson, Miller, and Hamrin note, "Most leadership theories do not see communication as constitutive of leadership, which is the position we take. Communication scholars, on the contrary, stress that leadership is enacted in communication processes."[39] In summary, leadership is listening.

Christian leadership communication skills are necessary to clearly communicate truth to a culture in fluidity. Postmodern culture is in dire need of a consistent message which can change lives and save souls. This message requires both a sender and a receiver to become efficacious. Whether the mode involves new media in its various forms, one-on-one dialogues, speeches to large groups, or the written word, it should always point to the gospel of Jesus Christ and the hope of glory. MacArthur writes, "If anything, the obligation to communicate the truth of the gospel clearly and accurately weighs more heavily on our generation than on those who have gone before us, because our opportunities are so much greater. Luke 12:48 says, 'From everyone who has been given much shall much be required.'"[40] MacArthur rightly points out that in this age, Christians have more resources available than in any time in history to present truth, and should use each of them for this purpose. Christian leaders living out their faith have a high calling and a great responsibility to know the truth and to present it in a manner which honors God. The authenticity of the message can only be found through a genuine messenger. MacArthur continues,

> As Christian communicators, we must commit ourselves to being what God has called us to be. We are not carnival barkers, used-car salesmen, or commercial pitchmen. We are Christ's ambassadors (2 Corinthians 5:20). Knowing the terror of the Lord (2 Corinthians 5:11), motivated by the love of Christ (2 Corinthians 5:14), utterly made new by Him (2 Corinthians 5:17), we implore sinners to be reconciled to God (2 Corinthians 5:20).[41]

According to Baldoni, "Effective messages are built upon trust. Trust is not something that we freely grant our leaders; we expect them to earn it. How? By demonstrating leadership in thought, word, and deed . . . Credibility is a

---

38. Mark 7:14.
39. Johansson et al., "Conceptualizing Communicative Leadership," 149.
40. MacArthur, "A Challenge for Christian Communicators," 8.
41. Ibid.

leader's currency. With it he or she is solvent; without it he or she is bankrupt. Communications reinforces a leader's credibility."[42] The credibility of the message largely depends on the reliability of the leader communicating the message. This should motivate the leader to live in a way which reflects the truth presented.

---

42. Baldoni, *Great Communication*, 4.

11

Epilogue

Those who lead disorderly lives tell those who are normal that it is they who deviate from nature, and think they are following nature themselves; just as those who are on board ship think that the people on shore are moving away. Language is the same everywhere; we need a fixed point to judge it. The harbour is the judge of those aboard ship, but where are we going to find harbour in morals? When everything is moving at once, nothing appears to be moving, as on board ship. When everyone is moving towards depravity, no one seems to be moving, but if someone stops, he shows up the others who are rushing on by acting as a fixed point.[1]

—BLAISE PASCAL

THE POSTMODERN ERA CREATED a new challenge for Christian leaders with its aversion to objective truth and its deconstruction and redefining of historically accepted terms. As God is immutable and his written word is not open to man's opinion, postmoderns see biblical Christianity as archaic and implausible. The inane nature of postmodern philosophy makes reason and logic quite difficult, as each person can establish his own truth and create new norms which may apply to only that individual. Each individual, in a sense, becomes his own God and creator of his own universe.

---

1. Pascal, *Pensees*, 383.

Unfortunately, this is a system designed to fail, as societies can only function on a sense of shared identity and purpose. Christian leaders need not fear this era and its entrapments, but instead must hold fast to what Pascal called the "fixed point."[2] Groothuis aptly notes,

> The fixed point in a shifting world is biblical truth and all that agrees with it, for "all truth is God's truth." Truth is rooted in God, who is "a mighty fortress, . . . a bulwark never failing" (Martin Luther). Those who have betrayed truth have joined the multitude that is moving toward depravity morally, intellectually, and spiritually—however contented and relevant these postmoderns may seem. By betraying the truth, they lose their voice, their authority, their endorsement by reality and their integrity. Humans, as finite and fallible beings, require a knowledge or reality outside of their cultures, languages and preferences in order to have any hope for moral, spiritual and intellectual repentance, restoration, and renewal. We must be true to the truth, developing the art and discipline of truthfulness in a world of untruth. The realities we autonomously construct are only unrealities, built on sand. In the end, God himself will deconstruct the sham deities. "Do people make their own gods? Yes, but they are not gods!" (Jer 16:20).[3]

Christian leaders, then, continually live their lives in alignment to the "fixed point" while leading this specious world to an abode of solace, rest, purpose, grace, and glory. The postmodern era, with its semblance of happiness, is instead empty and in need of substance. As this "fixed point" is truth, it must be defended, protected, and elevated regardless of the cost. Pascal writes, "And it is not obvious that, just as it is a crime to disturb the peace when truth reigns, it is also a crime to remain at peace when the truth is being destroyed. There is, therefore, a time when peace is just and a time when it is unjust."[4] When the world, like Pilate, asks "What is truth?", it is the responsibility of those who know this truth to unashamedly answer the inquiry.

The conscience of man informs him of the reality of God, making him accountable to the truth. The Apostle Paul makes this point clear in his letter to the church in Rome: "For what can be known about God is plain to them, because God has shown it to them. For his invisible attributes, namely, his eternal power and divine nature, have been clearly perceived, ever since the creation of the world, in the things that have been made.

2. Ibid.
3. Groothuis, *Truth Decay*, 265.
4. Pascal, *Pensees*, 346.

Epilogue

So they are without excuse."[5] The only remedy for unbelief is divine truth, and Christian leaders are commanded to know and present this truth in love. Regardless of vocation, leading by the sacrificial, *agape* love as taught and lived out in purity by Jesus Christ is the Christian's primary pursuit. The five "*Solas*" of the Reformation—*Sola Fide* (Faith alone), *Sola Scriptura* (Scripture alone), *Solus Christus* (Christ alone), *Sola Gratia* (Grace alone), and *Soli Deo Gloria* (Glory to God alone)—present a unique concatenation from which to lead. Although this current era and its fluid nature seem insurmountable, the challenge to truth is nothing new. Christian leaders must be the leaders of change in the postmodern era by leading with humility, mercy, and grace. Christocentric leadership requires courage, credibility, character, and compassion, as it reflects the very nature of Jesus Christ.

Although servant leadership has been pursued from a multitude of angles and attributes, only those aligned with the Bible are worthy of discussion and further research. In the Scriptures, many accounts are available which reveal the nature of godly leadership. In the Old and New Testament narratives and imperatives, a beautiful template for servant leadership has emerged in the written word. This Pauline pericope imperative sums up the basis for servant leadership with Christ as its core:

> Do nothing from rivalry or conceit, but in humility count others more significant than yourselves. Let each of you look not only to his own interests, but also to the interests of others. Have this mind among yourselves, which is yours in Christ Jesus, who, though he was in the form of God, did not count equality with God a thing to be grasped, but made himself nothing, taking the form of a servant, being born in the likeness of men.[6]

Although Greenleaf revived the discussion on servant leadership, its original basis is defined in the Scriptures and perfected in the person of Christ. Servant leadership is based on the idea that the follower is first. According to Northouse, "Putting others first is the sine qua non of servant leadership—the defining characteristic. It means using actions and words that clearly demonstrate to followers that their concerns are a priority, including placing followers' interests and success ahead of those of the leader."[7] Christian leadership and servant leadership are synonymous in their goals of serving others, even to the point of self-sacrifice.

5. Rom 1:19–20.
6. Phil 2:3–8.
7. Northouse, *Leadership*, 228.

Finally, communication is the only method available to reach the postmodern world with objective truth. The blessing of the current era is that many modes of communication exist through the insurgence of modern technology and social media. Each of these conduits provides an opportunity to reach people. Because these modes are also used by antithetical forces, it is incumbent upon Christian leaders to use them often to present the other side (truth) of the argument. Christian leaders are messengers of truth, whether in a secular work environment, in their community, in their homes, or in the church. Those called to this duty have a responsibility to communicate it well. The Apostle Paul expressed this need to communicate truth:

> How then will they call on him in whom they have not believed? And how are they to believe in him of whom they have never heard? And how are they to hear without someone preaching? And how are they to preach unless they are sent? As it is written, "How beautiful are the feet of those who preach the good news!" But they have not all obeyed the gospel. For Isaiah says, "Lord, who has believed what he has heard from us?" So faith comes from hearing, and hearing through the word of Christ.[8]

Although not all Christian leaders are "preachers," all are ambassadors of the Gospel and are called to communicate the "Good News" through actions and words. While the postmodern era is replete with the challenges of ambiguity, fluidity, and often travesty, Christian leaders can be agents of change by communicating objective truth to a world in desperate need of substance.

---

8. Rom 10:14–17.

Bibliography

"21.3 Percent of U.S. Population Participates in Government Assistance Programs Each Month." United States Census Bureau. https://www.census.gov/newsroom/press-releases/2015/cb15-97.html.

Alliance of Confessing Evangelicals. *The Cambridge Declaration*. Anaheim, CA: Alliance of Confessing Evangelicals, 1996.

Anderson, Walter Truett. *The Future of the Self: Inventing the Postmodern Person*. New York: Jeremy P. Tarcher, 1997.

Aristotle. *Metaphysics. Book IV*. Cambridge, MA: Harvard University Press, 1977.

Augustine, Marcus Dods, and Thomas Merton. *The City of God*. New York: Modern Library, 1950.

Baldoni, John. *Great Communication Secrets of Great Leaders*. New York: McGraw-Hill, 2003.

Barnes, Albert. "Section on 1 John 4:7." In *Notes on the New Testament*. http://www.ccel.org/print/barnes/ntnotes/xxvi.iv.vii.

Bauman, Zygmunt. "Foreword." In *Liquid Modernity*, 1. Malden, MA: Polity, 2012.

Beeke, Joel. "Christ Alone." *Tabletalk Magazine*, November 2012. http://www.ligonier.org/learn/articles/christ-alone/.

Beeke, Joel, and Randall J. Pederson. *Meet the Puritans: With a Guide to Modern Reprints*. Grand Rapids, MI: Reformation Heritage, 2006.

Berger, Travis A. "Servant Leadership 2.0: A Call for Strong Theory." *Sociological Viewpoints* (Fall 2014) 146–47. http://o-search.proquest.com.library.regent.edu/docview/1707097871?accountid=13479.

Berstene, T. C. "Resiliency—The Key to Embracing Change." *The Journal for Quality and Participation* 37, no. 2 (2014) 39–40. http://o-search.proquest.com.library.regent.edu/docview/1552784112?accountid=13479.

Blanchard, Ken, et al. *Leadership by the Book: Tools to Transform Your Workplace*. New York: William Morrow, 1999.

Bodie, Graham D. "The Active-Empathic Listening Scale (AELS): Conceptualization and Evidence of Validity Within the Interpersonal Domain." *Communication Quarterly* (2011) 277–97.

Boisselle, David. "Love, the Killer App, Works." *Inside Business*, April 2015. http://pilotonline.com/inside-business/news/columns/love-the-killer-app-works/article_413c306a-94c5-57b0-8a07-4705d8eba458.html.

Bibliography

Boje, David M., and Robert F. Dennehy. *Managing in the Postmodern World: America's Revolution Against Exploitation.* Dubuque, IA: Kendall, 1993.

Botha, Carolina S. "Teaching as an Act of Stewardship: Theology in Practice." *Hervormde Teologiese Studies* 70, no. 1 (2014) 1–5. http://o-search.proquest.com.library.regent.edu/docview/1680763839?accountid=13479.

Brown, John. *Hebrews.* London: Banner of Truth Trust, 1972.

Bucci, Joseph, and Paul W. Lewis. "The Case for Inclusion of Redemptive Managerial Dimensions in Servant Leadership Theory." *Journal of Biblical Integration in Business* 19, no. 1 (Fall 2016) 1–16.

Buchanan, James. *The Office and Work of the Holy Spirit.* 6th ed. New York: R. Carter, 1847.

Calvin, Jean, and J. T. MacNeill. *Institutes of the Christian Religion.* Vol. 1. London: SCM, 1961.

Campbell, David. "Good Leaders Are Credible Leaders." *Research Technology Management* 36, no. 5 (1993) 29. http://o-search.proquest.com.library.regent.edu/docview/213810008?accountid=13479.

Challies, Tim. "The Christian Conscience." http://www.challies.com/reading-classics-together/the-christian-conscience.

Clark, Gordon H. *Historiography: Secular and Religious.* Madison, WI: Trinity Foundation, 1994.

Condit, Bruce. "7 Critical Steps to Crisis Management." *Inc. Magazine,* October 2014. http://www.inc.com/bruce-condit/7-critical-steps-to-crisis-management.html.

Craige, Betty Jean. *Reconnection: Dualism to Holism in Literary Study.* Athens, GA: University of Georgia Press, 1988.

Dawkins, Richard. *A Devil's Chaplain: Reflections on Hope, Lies, Science, and Love.* Boston: Houghton Mifflin, 2003.

DelHousaye, Darryl, and Bobby Brewer. *Servant Leadership.* Scottsdale, AZ: SBC, 2004.

Denning, Stephen. *The Secret Language of Leadership: How Leaders Inspire Action Through Narrative.* San Francisco: Jossey-Bass, 2007.

———. "Why Leadership Storytelling Is Important." *Forbes,* June 2011. https://www.forbes.com/sites/stevedenning/2011/06/08/why-leadership-storytelling-is-important/#560of7ea78of.

Díez del Río, Isaías. "Postmodernidad Y Nueva Religiosidad." *Religion y Cultura* 39, no. 184 (1993) 55-91.

Dostoyevsky, Fyodor, and Ignat Avsey. *The Brothers Karamazov.* Oxford: New York, 1998.

Elwell, Walter A. "Compassion." In *Baker's Evangelical Dictionary of Theology.* https://www.biblestudytools.com/dictionaries/bakers-evangelical-dictionary/compassion.html.

Engstrom, Ted W. *The Making of a Christian Leader.* Grand Rapids, MI: Zondervan, 1976.

Fenner, William, and Edmund Calamy. *The Souls Looking-Glasse.* Cambridge, MA: Roger Daniel, 1640.

Ford, Leighton. *Transforming Leadership: Jesus' Way of Creating Vision, Shaping Values & Empowering Change.* Downers Grove, IL: Intervarsity, 1991.

Forlaron, Jim. "The Human Side of Change Leadership." *Quality Progress* 38, no. 4 (2005) 39–43.

Free Presbyterian Church. "Why Do the Five Solas Matter Today?" *Here We Still Stand* 5, no. 1 (June 2016) 28.

Fullan, Michael. *Leading in a Culture of Change.* San Francisco: Jossey-Bass, 2001.

Bibliography

Fuller, Thomas. *Gnomologia: Adagies and Proverbs; Wise Sentences and Witty Sayings, Ancient and Modern, Foreign and British.* London: B. Barker, 1732.

Gill, John. *Exposition of the Old and New Testament.* Streamwood, IL: Primitive Baptist Library, 1976. http://www.sacred-texts.com/bib/cmt/gill/joh013.htm.

Greenleaf, Robert K. *The Servant as Leader.* Indianapolis, IN: Robert K. Greenleaf Center, 1991.

Greenleaf, Robert K., and Larry C. Spears. *The Power of Servant-Leadership.* San Francisco: Berrett-Koehler, 1998.

Grenz, Stanley. *A Primer on Postmodernism.* Grand Rapids, MI: Eerdmans, 1996.

Groothuis, Douglas R. *Truth Decay: Defending Christianity Against the Challenges of Postmodernism.* Downers Grove, IL: InterVarsity, 2000.

———. "Why Truth Matters Most: An Apologetic for Truth-Seeking in Postmodern Times." *Journal of the Evangelical Theological Society* 47, no. 3 (2004) 441–54. http://o-search.proquest.com.library.regent.edu/docview/211146713?accountid=13479.

Grudem, Wayne. *Business for the Glory of God: The Bible's Teaching on the Moral Goodness of Business.* Wheaton, IL: Crossway, 2003.

Guinness, Os. *The American Hour: A Time of Reckoning and the Once and Future Role of Faith.* New York: Free Press, 1993.

Gwynne, S. C. *Rebel Yell: The Violence, Passion, and Redemption of Stonewall Jackson.* New York: Scribner, 2014.

Hackman, Michael Z., and Craig E. Johnson. *Leadership: A Communication Perspective.* 6th ed. Prospect Heights, IL: Waveland, 2013.

Harris, Robert. *The Works of Robert Harris: Revised, Corrected and Now Collected Into One Volume: With an Addition of Sundry Sermons: Some, Not Printed in the Former Edition: Others, Never Before Extant.* London: [James] Flesher, 1654.

Heft, James L. "The Courage to Lead." *Catholic Education: A Journal of Inquiry and Practice* 7, no. 3 (July 2013) 294–307. http://o-search.proquest.com.library.regent.edu/docview/1690500279?accountid=13479.

Henry, Carl F. H., ed. *Baker's Dictionary of Theology.* Grand Rapids, MI: Baker, 1973.

———. *God, Revelation and Authority.* Vol. 1. Waco: Word, 1976.

Henry, Matthew. *Matthew Henry's Concise Commentary on the Whole Bible.* Nashville: Thomas Nelson, 1997.

Hoffman, Louis. "Premodernism, Modernism, & Postmodernism: An Overview." http://postmodernpsychology.com/premodernism-modernism-postmodernism-an-overview/.

Hughes, Philip. *The Second Epistle to the Corinthians.* Vol. 9. *The New International Commentary on the New Testament.* Grand Rapids, MI: Eerdmans, 1962.

Hughes, Richard L., and Katherine Colarelli Beatty. *Becoming a Strategic Leader: Your Role in Your Organization's Enduring Success.* San Francisco: Jossey-Bass, 2005.

Johansson, Catrin, Vernon D. Miller, and Solange Hamrin. "Conceptualizing Communicative Leadership: A Framework for Analysing and Developing Leaders' Communication Competence." *Corporate Communications* 19, no. 2 (2014) 147–65. doi: http://o-dx.doi.org.library.regent.edu/10.1108/CCIJ-02-2013-0007.

Johnson, Terry L. *The Case for Traditional Protestantism: The Solas of the Reformation.* Edinburgh, UK: Banner of Truth Trust, 2004.

Jones, Jeffrey M. "Americans' Trust in Political Leaders, Public at New Lows." September 21, 2016. http://www.gallup.com/poll/195716/americans-trust-political-leaders-public-new-lows.aspx.

Bibliography

"Joni's Bio." *Joni and Friends.* http://www.joniandfriends.org/jonis-corner/jonis-bio/.

Kistemaker, Simon J. "Jesus as Story Teller: Literary Perspectives on the Parables." *The Master's Journal* 16, no. 1 (Spring 2005) 49–55.

Kotter, John P. *A Force for Change: How Leadership Differs from Management.* New York: Free Press, 1990.

Kuran, Evrim. "Leader as Storyteller." *Industrial and Commercial Training* 45, no. 2 (2013), 119–22. doi: http://o-dx.doi.org.library.regent.edu/10.1108/00197851311309561.

Laney, J. Carl. *John.* Chicago: Moody Bible Institute, 1992.

Lewis, C. S. *The Four Loves: C.S. Lewis.* Atlanta, Ga: Episcopal Media Center, 2000.

———. *Mere Christianity.* Glasgow, UK: Fount Paperbacks, 1977.

MacArthur, John. *1 Corinthians.* Chicago: Moody Bible Institute, 1984.

———. "A Challenge for Christian Communicators." *The Masters Seminary Journal* (Spring 2006) 7–15.

———. *Parables: The Mysteries of God's Kingdom Revealed Through the Stories Jesus Told.* Nashville: Thomas Nelson, 2015.

———. *The Pillars of Christian Character: The Basic Essentials of a Living Faith.* Wheaton, IL: Crossway, 1998.S

———. *The Truth War: Fighting for Certainty in an Age of Deception.* Nashville: Thomas Nelson, 2007.

———. *The Vanishing Conscience.* Dallas: Word Inc., 1994.

Marty, Martin. "Youth Between Late Modernity and Postmodernity." *Institute for Youth.* http://www.ptsem.edu/lectures/?action=tei&id=youth-1998-04.

Maxwell, John C. *The 21 Irrefutable Laws of Leadership: Follow Them and People Will Follow You.* Nashville: Thomas Nelson, 1998.

McCalman, James, and David Potter. *Leading Cultural Change: The Theory and Practice of Successful Organizational Transformation.* London: Kogan Page, 2015.

McKenzie, John L. *Dictionary of the Bible* 521. Milwaukee: Bruce, 1965.

Michael, Larry J. *Spurgeon on Leadership: Key Insights for Christian Leaders from the Prince of Preachers.* Grand Rapids, MI: Kregel, 2003.

Mohler, R. Albert. *The Conviction to Lead: 25 Principles for Leadership That Matters.* Minneapolis, MN: Bethany, 2012.

———. "What Is Truth? Truth and Contemporary Culture." *Journal of the Evangelical Theological Society* 48, no. 1 (2005) 63–75. http://o-search.proquest.com.library.regent.edu/docview/211152248?accountid=13479.

National Education Association. "Build Better Listening Skills: Now Hear This!" http://www.nea.org/tools/build-better-listening-skills.html.

Nel, Malan, and Eric Scholtz. "Calling, Is There Anything Special about It?" *Hervormde Teologiese Studies* 72, no. 4 (2016) 1–7. doi: http://o-dx.doi.org.library.regent.edu/10.4102/hts.v72i4.3183.

Nietzsche, Friedrich. "On Truth and Lie in an Extra-Moral Sense." New York: Viking, 1968.

Noebel, David A. *Understanding the Times: The Religious Worldviews of Our Day and the Search for Truth.* Eugene, OR: Harvest, 1994.

Northouse, Peter Guy. *Leadership: Theory and Practice.* Thousand Oaks, CA: Sage, 2004.

Packer, J. I. *Rediscovering Holiness.* Ann Arbor, MI: Vine, 1992.

Pascal, Blaise. *Pensees.* Paris: Librairie Generale Francaise, 1972.

Paton, Rob, and James McCalman. *Change Management: A Guide to Effective Implementation.* 3rd ed. London: Sage, 2000.

Bibliography

Paulien, Jon. *Everlasting Gospel, Ever-Changing World: Introducing Jesus to a Skeptical Generation.* Nampa, ID: Pacific, 2008.

Pearson, Christine M., and Judith A. Clair. "Reframing Crisis Management." *Academy of Management Review.* Vol. 23, no. 1 (Jan 1998).

Phillips, Timothy R., and Dennis L. Okholm. *Christian Apologetics in the Postmodern World.* Downers Grove, IL: InterVarsity, 1995.

Pink, A. W. *The Attributes of God.* Auckland, NZ: Floating Press, 2009.

Placher, William C., ed. "Callings: Twenty Centuries of Christian Wisdom on Vocation." Grand Rapids, MI: Eerdmans, 2005. Kindle edition.

Polletta, Francesca. "Storytelling in Politics." *Contexts* 7, no. 4 (Fall 2008) 26–31.

Rardin, Richard. *The Servant's Guide to Leadership.* Pittsburgh: Selah, 2001.

Reeder, Harry L., and Rod Gragg. *The Leadership Dynamic: A Biblical Model for Raising Effective Leaders.* Wheaton, IL: Crossway, 2008.

Roels, S. J. "The Christian Calling to Business Life." *Theology Today* 60, no. 3 (2003) 357–69. http://o-search.proquest.com.library.regent.edu/docview/208062545?accountid=13479.

Sarot, Marcel. "The Ultimate Miracle? The Historicity of the Resurrection of Jesus." *Hervormde Teologiese Studies* 70, no. 1 (2014) 1–9. http://o-search.proquest.com.library.regent.edu/docview/1680764051?accountid=13479.

Sayers, Dorothy L. *Creed or Chaos?* New York: Harcourt, 1949.

Selby, John Millin. *Stonewall Jackson as Military Commander.* London: Batsford, 1968.

Sendjaya, Sen, and James C. Sarros. "Servant Leadership: Its Origin, Development, and Application in Organizations." *Journal of Leadership & Organizational Studies* 9, no. 2 (Fall 2002) 57–64. http://o-search.proquest.com.library.regent.edu/docview/203144748?accountid=13479.

Spears, Larry C. "Character and Servant Leadership: Ten Characteristics of Effective, Caring Leaders." *The Journal of Virtues & Leadership* 1.1 (2010) 25–30.

Spears, Larry C., and Michele Lawrence. *Practicing Servant-Leadership: Succeeding Through Trust, Bravery, and Forgiveness.* San Francisco, CA: Jossey-Bass, 2004.

Spitz, Lewis W. *The Protestant Reformation 1517-1559.* New York: Harper & Row, 1985.

Sproul, R. C. *How Can I Develop a Christian Conscience?* Sanford, FL: Reformation Trust, 2013.

Spurgeon, Charles Haddon. "Love." https://www.spurgeon.org/resource-library/sermons/love#flipbook/

———. "The Need of Decision for the Truth." http://archive.spurgeon.org/s_and_t/truth.php.

———. "A Sermon (No. 229)." https://www.blueletterbible.org/Comm/spurgeon_charles/sermons/0229.cfm.

Strong, James. *The New Strong's Exhaustive Concordance of the Bible: With Main Concordance, Appendix to the Main Concordance, Key Verse Comparison Chart, Dictionary of the Hebrew Bible, Dictionary of the Greek Testament.* Nashville: Thomas Nelson, 1984.

Sullivan, John J. *Servant First! Leadership for the New Millennium.* Maitland, FL: Xulon, 2004.

Thomson, James. "Sola Scriptura." *The Presbyterian Record*, November 2011, 17–18. http://o-search.proquest.com.library.regent.edu/docview/906127242?accountid=13479.

Bibliography

Tribune News Services. "Disorientation Probable Cause Of Jfk Jr. Crash, Inquiry Finds." *Chicago Tribune*, July 7, 2000. http://articles.chicagotribune.com/2000-07-07/news/0007070267_1_spatial-disorientation-pilot-final-report.

van Dierendonck, Dirk. "Servant Leadership: A Review and Synthesis. Journal of Management." *Journal of Management* (2011) 1228–61.

van Dierendonck, Dirk, and Kathleen Patterson. "Compassionate Love as a Cornerstone of Servant Leadership: An Integration of Previous Theorizing and Research." *Journal of Business Ethics* 128, no. 1 (2015) 119–31. doi: http://o-dx.doi.org.library.regent.edu/10.1007/s10551-014-2085-z.

Veith, Gene Edward. *God at Work: Your Christian Vocation in All of Life*. Wheaton, IL: Crossway, 2002.

———. *Postmodern Times: A Christian Guide to Contemporary Thought and Culture*. Lexington, KY: Lexington Volunteer Recording Unit, 1998.

———. "Vocation: The Theology of the Christian Life." *Journal of Markets and Morality* 14, no. 1 (2011) 119–31. http://o-search.proquest.com.library.regent.edu/docview/1439118263?accountid=13479.

Vincent, Nathanael. *A Heaven or Hell Upon Earth, Or, a Discourse Concerning Conscience*. London: Thomas Parkhurst, 1676.

Voehl, Frank, and H. James Harrington. *Change Management: Manage the Change or It Will Manage You*. 2016.

Wald, Matthew L. "Safety Board Blames Pilot Error in Crash of Kennedy Plane - The New York Times." *The New York Times-Breaking News, World News & Multimedia*. Last modified July 7, 2000. http://www.nytimes.com/2000/07/07/nyregion/safety-board-blames-pilot-error-in-crash-of-kennedy-plane.html.

Watson, Thomas. *Discourses on Important and Interesting Subjects, Being the Select Works of the Rev. Thomas Watson*. Vols. I and II. N.p.: Blackie, Fullarton & Co. 1829.

———. *Heaven Taken by Storm*. N.p.: Bottom of the Hill, 2012.

Watson, Thomas, and Andrew Reilly. *A Body of Divinity*. Ashland, OR: Blackstone, 2016.

The Westminster Shorter Catechism. Edinburgh, Scotland: n.p., 1648. https://prts.edu/wp-content/uploads/2013/09/Shorter_Catechism.pdf.

White, Heath. *Postmodernism 101: A First Course for the Curious Christian*. Grand Rapids, MI: Brazos, 2006.

Williamson, G. I. *The Westminster Confession of Faith*. 2nd ed. New Jersey: P & R, 2004.

Witherington, Ben. *Work: A Kingdom Perspective on Labor*. Grand Rapids, MI: Eerdmans, 2011.

Zachman, Randall C. *The Assurance of Faith: Conscience in the Theology of Martin Luther and John Calvin*. Minneapolis, MN: Fortress, 1993.